Applied Linguistics and Language Study

GENERAL EDITOR : C. N. CANDLIN

English for Specific Purposes

A Case Study Approach

Edited by
R. MACKAY AND A. J. MOUNTFORD

LONGMAN

LONGMAN GROUP LIMITED
London

*Associated companies, branches and representatives
throughout the world*

This edition © Longman Group Ltd. 1978

First published 1978
Second impression 1979

ISBN 0 582 55090 4

Printed in Singapore by
New Art Printing Co Pte Ltd

Acknowledgements

We are grateful to the contributors whose work appears in this volume: those who agreed to allow us to reprint material, which constitutes Chapters 4 and 7, and particularly to those who wrote case studies especially for this volume: John Swales, Martin Bates, R. Straker Cook, James Morrison, R. R. Jordan, and C. N. Candlin, J. M. Kirkwood and H. M. Moore.

We would also like to thank the Centre for the Teaching of Foreign Languages (CELE) of the National Autonomous University of Mexico and the Regional Language Centre, (RELC) in Singapore for allowing us to reproduce the questionnaires in Chapter 2.

The conception and subsequent development of a collection such as this is rarely solely the results of the efforts of the authors and editors who produce the final version. Our gratitude is therefore extended to Dr Larry Selinker and Dr Jaroslav Peprnik who, however unwittingly, encouraged and nurtured the process of conception during English for Special Purposes seminars in Poznan, Poland in 1971 and Olomouc, Czechoslovakia in 1971, 1972 and 1973 respectively; to Maryse Bosquet and her two assistants Nathalie and Robert Fricot, for preparing the indexes, and to Professors Esther and James Taylor for providing the opportunity for most of the ideas in this collection to be taught to interested teachers during 1975 and 1976, in the Instituto Britannia, Mexico City.

R.M. and A.M.

We are grateful to Julius Groos Verlag KG for permission to reproduce a chapter from *International Review of Applied Linguistics in Language Teaching* Vol. XII/1.

Preface

The increasing specialisation of content in English teaching curricula since the early 1960s can be traced to a number of factors. The first is summed up in this analysis from an international meeting of specialists (held in London in December 1960) on second language learning as a factor in national development in Asia, Africa and Latin America:

> the language problem in development stems from at least three communication needs which are increasingly being recognised both in the developing countries themselves and in other countries aiding in their development: internal communication, transmission of science and technology, and international communication

The analysis is significant for its concentration on the concept of 'communication need', implying a specification of purposes for the learning of language as communication. Such a need for a specification was in itself novel to ELT course planning and materials design at the time, as the textbooks of the era exemplify. Moreover the suggestion that English teaching could be bound up with the teaching of other subjects in the school or post-school curriculum offered the possibility not only of a particular role for English as a vehicle for transmitting knowledge, as a means rather than an end in itself, but also an attractive source of language data for course planners, and potentially an injection of novel methodologies for teachers.

The second factor is a happy coincidence to the first; the 1960s saw a recrescence of interest in the study of language in social contexts associated in particular with the anthropological and ethnographic work of sociolinguists like Labov, Hymes and Gumperz, concerned not only to specify the components of speech events, but in so doing to demonstrate a workable methodology. A growing concern for the specification of particular communicative needs by commissioners of ELT programmes, supported by understandable cries for relevance by students, could thus be satisfied by applied linguistic research, able to collect data, analyse them sociolinguistically and design appropriate courses and materials.

It was, however, perhaps to be expected that early attempts to specify the 'English for Science' would go little further than fitting a general, non-subject-specific 'technical' lexis to a similar range of structure as was available in the non-technical general course. The then popular term 'register' fitted in nicely, and gradually empirical research into the structures and vocabulary of scientific and technical specialisms (cf. in particular the 1968 OSTI Report) led to materials which displayed in a most useful way the lexical and structural identity of a variety of sub-branches of science and technology. Although the differences in structure that were isolated were fewer than one might have at the outset imagined, it was clear that English for Science and Technology could not merely replace 'orange' by 'Bunsen burner' in the 'This is a . . .' structure of lesson 1.

It is here that a third factor emerges, itself also represented in the opening analysis. Developments in linguistics itself, or more especially in associated disciplines such as sociology, social psychology and philosophy, suggested that a view of language as communication could not easily be adequately contained in the form-oriented sentence-based linguistics of the time. Understanding utterances as a pragmatic achievement compelled a view of language in discourse terms where what was needed was an examination of the concepts and values underlying sentence-meaning, and, moreover, the processes adopted by interlocutors in conveying and understanding messages. Once again this shift found a ready response in designers and writers of specialist materials. Rather than looking at the formal registers of science and technology as merely a collection of specialist lexis and structure, what was needed was accounts of the ways the reasoning and conceptual processes of 'doing science' were reflected in language choice. Aided in part by 19th century work on rhetoric, philosophical studies into speech act theory, and ethno-methodological accounts of discourse structure, it now seemed possible to suggest that there might be much more common ground than had been realised between the practice of scientific and technological subjects in the L_1 and the L_2. If it could be shown that these concepts, reasoning processes and discourse structures were common to the speakers of different languages, as far as talking about and doing science and technology was concerned, then in teaching English in such a context one might be involving specialist learners in performing in the target language communicative tasks already familiar to them from their subject work in their mother tongue. In Selinker and Trimble's terms:

'Generally, foreign language learning is considered as subject-matter, with no specific goal for using the language. We . . . cannot take that position at all . . . our students are learning a foreign language primarily in order to manipulate difficult intellectual material in it'

What, then, are the current implications of these interrelating factors for ESP course design?

1 A view of language as communication implies teaching materials which interrelate form, function and strategy, in a methodology which promotes participation by the learner in the process of interpreting meanings.

2 Given that the ESP learner sees English as a means to the pursuit of academic or vocational goals, and not as an end in itself, analysis of the specific communicative implications of these goals is a necessary point of departure.

3 These restricted objectives and the link to subject matter highlight the integrative place of English and the English teacher in the general curriculum of the institution or the processes of the job.

4 The processes of data collection, discourse analysis and didacticisation suggest a unified applied linguistic methodology for ESP course designers, despite the apparent heterogeneity of their communicative purposes.

5 The extension of 'special purpose language' beyond registerial differences of lexis and structure towards universalist ideas of concepts and reasoning processes may suggest that the much emphasised distinctions between ESP and 'general' ELT are inappropriate and counterproductive.

The value of this contribution to the *Applied Linguistics and Language Study Series* lies in the answers and relevant discussion of the above points, provided by the wide-ranging collection of papers and the coherent editorial introductions of the editors. Part One of the collection, *The Problem Surveyed*, examines the sociological, linguistic, psychological and pedagogic design factors that ESP has to reflect, while offering a clear account of one of the ways learners' communicative needs can be assessed. Part Two, *Approaches to ESP Textbook Design*, not only gives interesting insights into the background to writing ESP materials, but in the article by Allen and Widdowson outlines that view of language as communication in ESP to which I refer earlier. Perhaps of most value to the course designer and materials writer, however, is the final Part Three, where the editors have collected a variety of Case Studies. These not only provide practical illustration of underlying principles, but can act as useful models.

Above all, however, the articles have a 'defining' and 'standard-establishing' effect. They make clear, firstly, that ESP should remain loyal to collected rather than invented data; that 'special purposes' involve not only specialisation in form and discourse but also in skills and tasks; that with a content appropriately bought in from the subject of study or work, its methodology implies an increasing general concern for learner-centredness reflected, desirably, in a closeness of work cycles and study cycles not hitherto attainable in global and general course materials. Secondly, in terms of standards, the question can reasonably be asked whether the above are not in any case desiderata for course design; why limit their applicability to *special purposes*? Ought it not to be axiomatic that in teaching 'general' conversational strategies we begin by analysing conversational structure; that in teaching 'general' writing skills we analyse written discourse, that the 'work' of understanding actual discourse be reflected in classroom interpretive procedures? Is there any case, then, for not applying the criteria we rightly apply to ESP materials, as suggested in this collection, to ELT materials at large? To do so would at very least dramatically reduce the sociolinguistic implausibility of much accepted and current language teaching material, and bring the world of representation closer to the actuality of communication.

Christopher N. Candlin, *August 1977*
General Editor

Contents

xi

xii

PART ONE

The Problem Surveyed

The two chapters in this part are introductory in two ways. Firstly, they introduce the reader to the theme of the book – the teaching of English for Special Purposes – by distinguishing those features that make it different from the teaching of General English. Secondly, they introduce the reader to particular theoretical and practical issues that are taken up in other papers in the book, particularly Chapters 3 and 10. The particular requirements of learners that have led to the need for a different response by teachers and materials designers are discussed, together with the notions that lie behind such responses – the renewed interest in language as communication, and the movement away from structural/behaviourist methodological models, for example. In addition, the importance of being clear about the nature of the learners' needs is stressed, through a questionnaire or by structured interview. It will be seen that ESP does not represent any new body of dogma as such, but is essentially a pragmatic response to a developing situation in which the many reasons that learners have for learning English are made amenable to more systematic description so that relevant and more effective materials can be prepared for teachers to use. In this sense, then, *special* should be construed as *more specific*, with a shift of emphasis in ELT syllabus planning towards the learner's *purpose*, allied to a growing awareness of the importance of the relationship between language and other areas of the learners' curriculum and/or activities.

1

The Teaching of English for Special Purposes: Theory and Practice

R. MACKAY AND A. J. MOUNTFORD

1 English Language Teaching and English for Special Purposes

Over the last ten years or so the term 'languages for special purposes' has appeared frequently in the literature relating to English language teaching. It is generally used to refer to the teaching of English for a clearly utilitarian purpose. This purpose is usually defined with reference to some occupational requirement, e.g. for international telephone operators, civil airline pilots etc., or vocational training programmes, e.g. for hotel and catering staff, technical trades etc., or some academic or professional study e.g. engineering, medicine, law, etc. This 'field' of English language teaching possesses two important characteristics which influence profoundly the methodology not only of materials production but of classroom activity: firstly, the close association of special purpose language teaching with adult learners, or, at least, learners at the post-secondary level of general education; and secondly, the important auxiliary role that the English language is called upon to play in such cases. Language learners require English as a means of furthering their specialist education or as a means of performing a social or working role, that is, a working role as a scientist, technologist, technician, etc. efficiently.

1.1 *Aims of Foreign Language Learning*

When English as a Foreign Language is taught to children at the primary and early secondary levels of education, it is generally taught with a general educational aim in mind – that is, it is regarded as a 'good thing' for them to learn a foreign language as a part of a broad education. There is usually, however, no immediate and specific requirement for such children to make use of the language in any communicative situation. The purpose of learning the language is essentially a 'deferred' purpose, deferred till the tertiary level of education, normally at University, where, it is agreed, a knowledge of

English would be helpful in their academic studies. Immediate aims of learning English are defined by the requirements of examinations. Inevitably what is taught to primary and secondary level children is not a communicative knowledge of English language use, but a knowledge of how the syntactic and lexical rules of English operate. The language system is taught, suitably contextualised, by means of systematic audio-lingual drill and exercise techniques based on habit formation theory of learning and a structuralist description of English. This may be an effective manner of teaching English usage – the rules of syntactic arrangement in sentences – but it is less certain that an understanding of how these rules are related to language in use for communicative purposes is an automatic result of this instruction.

What the thousands of children succeed in learning in this way is what is necessary in order to pass examinations. Whether such examinations accurately reflect the uses to which English will be put at the tertiary level is another matter altogether. Adults, on the other hand, unless they are learning a foreign language for 'pleasure' at evening institutes, as a 'cultural' and social experience, are generally highly conscious of the use to which they intend to put it. That use is frequently associated with an occupational, vocational, academic or professional requirement; without a knowledge of the foreign language, their development in their chosen sphere of work could be restricted or at least adversely affected.

When needs are clear, learning aims can be defined in terms of these specific purposes to which the language will be put, whether it be reading scientific papers or communicating with technicians on an oil rig. The result is that almost immediately, teaching can be seen to be effective in that the learner begins to demonstrate communicative ability in the required area. Thus, it is the essential auxiliary role that English is called upon to play, particularly at the tertiary level of education, that is a prime motivating factor. Where such a requirement for a communicative ability is matched with specially designed materials relevant to the needs of particular students the results can be impressive. But where the language courses at the tertiary level merely repeat the content and techniques of those at the secondary level – with emphasis on the teaching of grammatical structure and lexical items in exercises that do little more than manipulate linguistic forms – the results are unlikely to be any more effective than they were before. Moreover students become disillusioned with the value of such instruction and increasingly sceptical of their capacity to learn the language. This latter situation is, unfortunately, all too prevalent. On the one hand, little adjustment is made to the nature of the learning materials or the teaching method to accommodate the particular cognitive skills and learning ability of adults; on the other hand, little attempt is made to relate the teaching materials to either the communicative requirement or the learners' subject specialisations. Thus, the ELT courses offered are neither cognisant of the learners maturity nor relevant to their social role. More of the same as before is likely to be no more effective than it was before. A difference in approach from the current 'start at the beginning again', or remedial 'solutions' is needed when English ceases to be an examination subject and assumes the role of instrument of communication.

To meet this situation acronymic variants of general ELT have arisen: ESP (English for Special Purposes) and EST (English for Science and Technology). But even such terms are indeed now too general. We now talk in terms of 'English in Workshop Practice' or 'English in Agricultural Science', indicating the field of study being dealt with; or we can talk of 'English for Academic Purposes' (EAP) and 'English for vocational or occupational purposes' (EOP) indicating generally the nature of the purpose involved.

1.2 *Special Purposes and Special Languages*

At this point an important distinction needs to be made: English for Special Purposes implies a special *aim*. This aim may determine the precise area of language required, skills needed and the range of functions to which language is to be put. But it need not imply a special *language*. 'It is easy to confuse the idea of a special language (or segment of a language) with that of specialised aim.' (Perren, 1974). Clearly the two notions interlock, but they need to be discussed separately.

The only practical way in which we can understand the notion of 'special language' is as a restricted repertoire of words and expressions selected from the whole language because that restricted repertoire covers every requirement within a well-defined context, task or vocation. Thus, for example, the language of international air-traffic control could be regarded as 'special', in the sense that the repertoire required by the controller is strictly limited and can be accurately determined situationally, as might be the linguistic needs of a dining-room waiter or air-hostess. However, such restricted repertoires are not languages, just as a tourist phrase book is not a grammar. Knowing a restricted 'language' would not allow the speaker to communicate effectively in novel situations, or in contexts outside the vocational environment. Indeed there are very few contexts for which a restricted repertoire is entirely satisfactory. The 'language' used in banking or veterinary medicine or naval architecture have occasionally been talked about as 'special languages'. However this is misleading. They are in no way analogous to restricted repertoires. Certainly they demonstrate certain vocabulary items which do not occur in other fields, but their syntax is not restricted in any way. An exponent in any of these fields requires as much of resources of the English language as is being used in this book, for example. It is misleading therefore to regard such particular usages or particular uses 'special language'. This would imply a discreteness for these fields separating one off from another, and isolating all of them from some equally discrete entity known as General English. This is manifestly not the case. What we have is the same language employed for similar and different uses employing similar and different usages.

Thus, the notion of 'special language' should best be interpreted as 'restricted repertoire'. Unfortunately, the notion has been more widely interpreted in the sense of English for Special Purposes being concerned with the teaching of a special language as a statistically quantifiable 'register' defined in terms of formal linguistic properties, lexical items, collocations and sentence structures. The result has been that conventional structural approaches to syllabus design have been applied to a more restricted sample of language data. ESP and EST are regarded as different from general ELT *only* in terms of the former being associated with samples of language taken from subject-specific sources. Thus, the approach is the same to data that is conceived as different in statistically identified ways through word counts and structure counts. We would maintain, however, that what is needed for ESP is a difference in approach to data that is conceived not as fundamentally different in terms of linguistic usages – though clearly particular items and patterns can be identified as specific to particular subject specialisations or vocational/occupational roles – but which represents particular modes of language use that characterise science in general or occupational/vocational uses of language in particular.

The emphasis of the word 'special' then, in English for Special Purposes should be firmly placed upon the *purpose* of the learner for learning the language, not on the language he is learning. What constitutes language variation is the use to which language is put in particular circumstances by particular users. Hence, identifying homogeneous groups of language users and characterising their uses of language in particular circumstances together with a representative selection of linguistic usages habitually employed, would be a productive procedure to adopt. This is preferable to starting out with a study of the language system characteristic of an *ad hoc* selection of physics texts or banking texts, etc., and trusting that through the teaching of such usage in conventional exercises particular groups of learners will infer how to use language communicatively in situations where they have to 'do' physics or banking as physicists or bankers.

2 Teaching English to Scientists and Technologists (EST)

We have identified English for Science and Technology (EST) as a major sub-division of the 'field of teaching English for Special Purposes' (ESP). We can now consider the principal factors involved in designing course materials relevant to learners in the fields of science or technology. First, we shall consider the role of English for non-native speaking scientists and technologists, and having done that we will specify the factors involved in the design and planning of courses. The first major step is to identify the needs of the specific group of learners and the educational and curriculum setting into which teaching of English must fit. Such information is essential as a background to the more directly linguistic considerations affecting course content. That is, we cannot decide what we are going to teach until we know to whom and why teaching is required.

2.1 *The Role of English*

There can be no disputing the need for English by students of scientific disciplines. English is now established as the principal international language of science. As long ago as 1957 UNESCO reported that nearly two-thirds of engineering literature appears in English but more than two-thirds of the world's professional engineers cannot read English. This has meant that not only are undergraduates all over the world obliged to read an increasing proportion of textbooks in English but also that 'success in graduate work is becoming more and more related to the ability to read the appropriate literature in English and to take part in international conferences where the greater part of the contracts take place through the medium of English' (Ewer and Latorre, 1967).

A basic distinction needs to be made between English as a main study language, i.e. as a medium for science instruction, and English as an additional study language, i.e. in an auxiliary but necessary support role. Clearly where all science is taught in English, e.g. that situation facing foreign students studying in an English speaking country, a considerably higher standard of language proficiency is needed in order for students to comprehend and manipulate difficult intellectual material. In such situations success or failure in science is in large measure a consequence of success or failure in English. On the other hand, where English has an auxiliary role the motivation to learn the language is nowhere near as strong, particularly where the efforts of up to six years of learning English at the secondary level have resulted in only a minimal ability to use and understand the language. Frequently, also, in this situation it is common to find the aims and methods of the English language department at variance with the requirements of science and technology departments, the former still concerned with drilling conversational English and manipulating structural patterns while the latter require swift and effective reading skills. But in both these situations, there is a need to see the role of English basically in terms of its providing accessibility to knowledge contained in textbooks, periodicals and journals, reports and abstracts. That is to say that the role of English is associated with particular uses of English to extract information, interpret data and theories, report on latest advances, etc. in particular areas of specialist knowledge. Such uses of language in science can be associated with particular scientific concepts and methods of enquiry. Thus, there is obvious common sense in seeing the role of English at the tertiary level in association with particular specialist subject areas. The teaching and learning of English can, and should ideally, be seen as a set of integrated activities in both mediums and auxiliary language situations.

2.2 Design Factors in EST Courses

The factors involved in designing EST courses can be classified under four headings: sociological, linguistic, psychological and pedagogic.

2.2.1 SOCIOLOGICAL FACTORS

The initial step is to acquire information about the kind of learner for whom the programme is to be developed and the uses to which he will be required to put English. Thus accurate data relating to age, previous experience of the target language, and the learner's specialisation and attainment within it can be gathered by standard sampling techniques and the administration of a carefully planned questionnaire. In a similar way data concerning his exact needs, the uses to which he is required to put the language, must be gathered. Chapter 2 deals in some detail with some of the important procedures involved in gathering this basic but essential information. In many cases courses which purport to teach 'English for Businessmen', 'French for Engineers', 'German for Chemists' etc. have failed because they were not based on an identification of the actual uses to which language was required to be put by such learners. The traditional division of language skills into listening, speaking, reading and writing are not usually delicate enough to provide an accurate description of the learner's needs. More will be said of this later under pedagogic factors.

2.2.2 LINGUISTIC FACTORS

The selection of the linguistic content of the language to be used for particular purposes depends on an adequate and appropriate description of the language characteristic of that which the learner is required to handle. By appropriate description we mean one which not only takes account of the code features of the language system but the communicative features of language use. Such a description cannot be arrived at merely by making inventories of items found in selected texts. Such lists however can be utilised to ensure that particular code features are focussed on in the materials – features of syntax and lexis that typify the communicative patterns such as defining, describing, explaining, classifying, making deductions, hypotheses, etc. which are found to be characteristic of that particular type of text.

2.2.3 PSYCHOLOGICAL FACTORS

Course materials that are designed within a framework of structural linguistics tend to employ the operational tenets of behaviourist learning theory. This involves an emphasis on the formation of 'correct' habits, the ability to compose correct sentences through a knowledge of the language system for which drills and exercises are devised. This is usually achieved by a situational presentation in order to make the language meaningful. This step is then followed by repetition type exercises to master the rule in question. The emphasis is thus on usage, i.e. on the teaching of the structural characteristics of the language system. It is increasingly being recognised, however, that skill in using the language as a means of communication is not necessarily a consequence of learning it as a formal system. The assumption of the structuralist/behaviorist approach – and one that is widely prevalent – indeed, the standard conventional approach of general ELT – is that once the structural characteristics of scientific or technical English are mastered the students will automatically be able to recognise and use the characteristic communicative patterns of scientific or technological enquiry. The evidence is that this does not happen. What appears to be required is an approach that focusses attention on the learning of the language as a communicative instrument from the learner's point of view. This approach emphasises the 'problem solving' role of the learner as a participant in the interpretation and composition of discourse.

By taking advantage of what the learner already knows, from study in his own language, about the organisation of scientific discourse and the way in which scientific procedures are represented in language, the teacher can lead the learner to an understanding of how scientific communication in English handles these functions. This implies, firstly, a shift in emphasis away from assessment of a learner's linguistic knowledge in terms of what he has failed to learn earlier, towards the effective communicative use he can make of what he has learned. Secondly, it involves making clear the distinction between testing on the one hand, and exercising knowledge on the other. In particular, teaching and testing are confused with regard to the skill of comprehension. Asking a learner questions on the content of a written or spoken text may test whether comprehension has taken place. There is no real evidence to indicate that such a procedure is a valid or effective way of teaching comprehension or exercising strategies and techniques for understanding.

2.2.4 PEDAGOGIC FACTORS

We must be clear about what language skills are being focussed on or need to be focussed on, in order to devise pedagogic procedures that will actually develop such skills. We have already noted that the traditional division of language skills is not sufficiently delicate to enable us to describe accurately the learner's needs. Particular tasks requiring certain functional skills must be listed, e.g. abstracting technical articles, monitoring radio broadcasts, taking an active part in oral seminars, report writing based on experimental procedures, reading instructional material to supplement information gained in the L_1 etc. Jordan and Mackay (1973) describe in considerable detail the functional skills employed by overseas postgraduate students studying in the U.K. Universities. The possession of accurate, objective information about the learner, his specialism and his needs, enables the course planner to narrow down the area of language use and usage – and of course the mode, spoken or written – from which the linguistic items in communicative patterns of language use should be drawn. For example, a doctor working with patients in a foreign language might be required to interview and understand patients, give instructions to nurses, converse with colleagues about particular cases, write up case studies, read highly technical descriptions of systems and treatments in manuals published by firms and organisations marketing pharmaceutical products. Course materials to cater for such specific requirements would have to be pedagogically organised to relate the appropriate language skills together in an ordered and situationally relevant manner in units of teaching material.

Materials which have been prepared without the learner group's characteristics having been taken into consideration, based on unsuitable or irrelevant samples of language and units of description, will have low motivational value for the student. It is important that classroom methodology be evolved to cater for the specific motivation and intellectual maturity of the kind of learner who is adding a foreign language to a scientific or technological training.

Design factors in EST course materials preparation may be summarised in terms of answers to the following questions:

Sociological: What are the characteristics of the learner and what are the learner's requirements for learning the language?

Linguistic: What kind of descriptive apparatus is appropriate to account for the language used by scientists and technologists?

Psychological: Orientation to what theory of learning is appropriate in EST to reflect our concern with the teaching of communicative as well as linguistic competence?

Pedagogic: What skills are to be taught, in what order, and how are the relationships between skills to be authentically presented and practised?

2.3 *The Role of the L₁*

We need now to consider the role of the L_1 in relation to the need to provide foreign students of science and technology with access to knowledge in their specialist fields of study. There are two ways in which the L_1 can function: as the language into which information written or spoken in English is translated; or in support of the L_2 language learning operation.

2.3.1 TRANSLATION

Texts requiring translation vary 'not only as regards their special subject content but also as regards types of document, each type calling for more or less different treatment.' (UNESCO, 1957.) The following categories may serve as examples:

'Presentation of new knowledge and descriptions of its application in practice: papers in the proceedings of learned societies and technical institutions. University theses. Longer reports.

Integrations and reviews of existing knowledge and experience: articles in scientific and technical journals. Separate pamphlets and reports. Reference manuals.

Educational material: syllabuses, certificates and diplomas. Textbooks. Popular science publications.

Documents relating to engineering and industrial applications: contracts and specifications for works. Reports on tests and analyses. Trade catalogues, publicity and directories. Patent specifications. National standards and international standardising recommendations.' (UNESCO, 1957.)

These examples of the kind of texts that require translation suggest that the need to teach foreign students of science and technology to read English efficiently arises basically because of the failure of a translation programme to cope with the needs of practising scientists. The 'failure' should be judged very relatively indeed: relative to the amount and range of information which is produced each year, and the number of languages into which it would need to be translated and the number of translators that would be required not only adequately conversant with the subject specialism and the conventions of the kinds of discourse found within such subjects (see the categories above), but also having a near native-speaker like competence in English. For, as the UNESCO report from which we have been quoting goes on to say,

> '... specialised translating involves much more than the mechanical looking up of "equivalents" of the special terms in dictionaries ... it is, or should be axiomatic that no body can properly translate what he does not understand; hence satisfactory technical translating can only be done by someone with the requisite technical knowledge and practice in technical reasoning, to follow technical arguments in the required speciality and to bridge over gaps in such an argument. The kind of competence required to do this depends not only on the nature and subject matter of the original text, but also on the purpose of the translation and on the kind of reader for whom it is intended.
>
> In order to translate papers written by and intended for scientists engaged in original research at the frontiers of knowledge, the translator must himself be familiar with those frontiers.'
>
> (UNESCO, 1957–27.)

In view of the expensive, slow and uncertain process of translation it is hardly surprising that translation programmes in developing countries, in particular, are able to no more than scratch the surface of the problem of making available to scientists the information they require. On the other hand, the use for English as a medium of instruction is often a political decision of some consequence, even at the tertiary level, and may not be countenanced at the secondary level. Despite the expansion of education at the tertiary level and the recognised need to train scientists and technologists, a similar investment of money and effort has not gone into translation services. Thus, dependence on English, reluctantly in some cases, either as a medium or *de facto* medium or as an auxiliary service language, is unavoidable at the higher levels of scientific education.

2.3.2 THE L₁ IN TEACHING

The assumed disadvantages of using the student's (L_1) as a teaching aid in English Language teaching are constantly being pointed out. It is argued that it interferes with the processes of achieving fluency in English and encourages a continued dependency upon the L_1 as the mediator between the mental encoding or decoding of messages and the target language. However it is true that where the role of English is that of auxiliary to specialist studies, particularly in tertiary

education and in an EFL situation, the information the student gains
from reading English texts is required to be at his disposal in his L_1
only. That is, although the information presented to him is in English,
when he is required to recall or produce it, he does so in his mother
tongue. In EFL situations, tutorials, discussions, examination
questions and dissertations are written, not in English, but in the
student's L_1.

Hence 'translation' of a particular kind can be a useful pedagogic
tool in an EST Programme. This particular kind of 'translation' has
been called 'information transfer' (Allen and Widdowson, 1974: see
Chapter 3). It is based on the fact that the processes and procedures of
science are the same no matter what the mother tongue of the scientist
concerned. Likewise, scientific discourse represents a way of
conceptualising reality and a way of communicating which must, if it
is to remain scientific, be independent of different languages and
different cultures. Students of or professionals in the various
branches of science and technology are already familiar with the
procedures of their field and the manner in which communication in
their specialisms are organised. The task of the English programme
is, therefore, by taking advantage of this knowledge, to demonstrate
to them how these procedures and principles of communicative
organisation are realised in English. What is understood traditionally
by 'translation', that is the reproducing, word for word and sentence
for sentence, of Text A in Language 1 as Text B in Language 2, does
not consciously take advantage of this knowledge of the way in which
scientific communication is organised. Hence, not being able to see
the wood for the trees, the student stumbles on problems and
difficulties in the surface structures and lexical items. The result, as
every teacher knows, is not a re-creation of the information contained
in the original text, but a mangled version of the surface structures.

Information transfer, or re-creation of information, on the other
hand, does not involve a direct movement from a text in one language
to a text in the other. It is a three cornered operation making use of
non-verbal or partly-verbal representations of information, such as

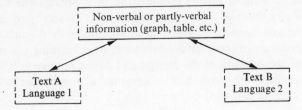

graphs, tables, diagrams, flow charts and illustrations. This can be represented diagrammatically, see p. 13.

When the non-verbal information is accompanied by text in English, then the task the student must perform is that of comprehension– re-creation of the information in his L_1. When the non-verbal information is accompanied by text in the L_1 then the task would be one of composition – re-creation of the information in English:

Comprehension

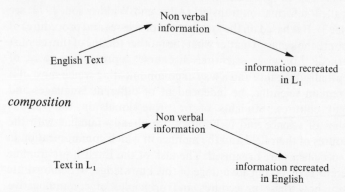

composition

The role of the L_1 has been discussed in both a negative and an affirmative way: on the one hand, the impossibility of the L_1 providing translation of *sufficient* information pertaining to scientists and technologists to enable them to 'do' science without recourse to a foreign language, the most useful of which is English: on the other hand, the teaching of English in association with non-verbal modes of communication. Where translation can be employed as a pedagogic procedure, it provides an opportunity for students to relate their own knowledge of science – gained in their own language where it has been used to instruct them in science – to the acquisition of English as a foreign or second language. Such an association may not only be pedagogically useful; it may have a political and cultural significance of some importance. For in many countries there may exist a negative attitude to English on the grounds that it supplants the L_1 in a particularly sensitive area, namely school and university education. With the overthrow of the grammar translation method – undeniably an impediment to successful second language learning – went the sense of the equality of the foreign and native language. With the introduction of 're-creation of information' as a technique in EST a balance can be restored.

3 Approaches to EST Materials Design

3.1 *Linguistics and Language Teaching*

The development of interest over the past few years in EST has coincided with an increasing interest by linguists, as a result of work in the fields of sociolinguistics and philosophy, in the communicative properties of language use. These developments are not unconnected; they derive ultimately from a recognition that a model of language as a formal system is not sufficient to account for how language users use language to communicate. This has always been a tenet of the London School of Linguistics and continued to be upheld by Prof. Michael Halliday even at the height of transformational generative euphoria. The special purpose of EST at the tertiary level has been directed towards enabling students to use their knowledge of English in order to further their knowledge of specialist subjects. But although the need for effective EST programmes has been recognised and articulated, the methodology and materials have not been sufficiently focussed on the problems of teaching and learning language as a means of communication.

One of the reasons for this is the relationship that exists between linguistics and language teaching. The language teacher has traditionally looked to the linguist and grammarian for guidance. He has adopted the linguist's categories of language description and used them as categories of instruction. What the linguist has not described, the teacher has not taught. The dearth of materials for the advanced learner dealing with units of language larger than the sentence testifies to this. Only recently has the linguist begun to show a sustained interest in language as communication. But even this development does not automatically mean that the language teacher now has a clear lead to follow. The goals of the linguist and the language teacher are vastly different. The former has as his aim the provision of a systematic and exhaustive linguistic description of the language.

What we are saying, in effect, is that the language teacher does not necessarily have to wait for the linguist to furnish him with insights or erect a finished model which the applied linguist may only then try to apply to language teaching problems. 'The language teacher,' Widdowson (1975) points out, 'should be adept at drawing insights from a wide spectrum of enquiry and to exploit them for his own purposes in order to arrive at a synthesis based on pedagogic principles.' This eclecticism has not always been so strongly advocated. Most teaching materials produced for general ELT, and also for EST, have been bound up closely with a particular model of description of the language system and the patterning of its surface structure. In the absence of clear cut directives from linguistics, itself a subject in a state of flux, ELT methodology for science and technology has tended not to create the synthesis of linguistic insights necessary for an eclectic model, but has fallen back on the traditional model and gone no further than linguistic descriptions afforded by a structuralist approach. But such a model emphasises usage and not use, sentence level description rather than inter-sentence relations, and the statistical significance of lexical items rather than their communicative value as instances of use.

3.2 *Theory and Practice in the Past*

As we have already noted, the theoretical base underlying much of the material already produced for EST is the notion of register, of formally differentiated and distinct sub-codes of a particular language.

> 'In accordance with this view of functional variation language teachers engaged in preparing English material for students of science and technology and other specialist areas of use have supposed their task involves simply the selection and presentation of those lexical and syntactic features which occur most commonly in passages of English dealing with the specialist topics their students are concerned with.' (Widdowson, 1974.)

The kind of materials that such an approach results in are typified by Ewer and Latorre's *Basic Scientific English* (1969). The procedure for the design of EST courses that they adopt can be summarised as follows:

> '(a) analyses of the English actually used in the "target" conditions; (b) selection of the most frequently-occurring or useful items in relation to the teaching time available; (c) systematic exercising and drilling of this material in contexts reflecting the special interests of the learners; (d) the provision of supplementary readings from the corresponding literature.'
> (Ewer and Latorre, 1967, p. 229.)

Ewer has been at pains elsewhere to emphasise 'the wide variations in lexis between the typical school course and that of the basic language of scientific literature ... and that discrepancies of a comparable degree also exist in grammar.' (Ewer, 1971, p. 67.) Materials based on such an approach undoubtedly can serve some of the language needs of the students for which they are intended, those which have to do with a knowledge of the code features of the language system. However they do not seem to provide systematically for other needs which have to do with an understanding of the communicative functioning of the language.

While Ewer and Latorre adopt a 'discrete item' approach, and rehearse the familiar paradigm of tense usage and structural patterns, the approach employed by Herbert (1965) varies at particular points significantly. Although he is conscious of the importance of vocabulary items and verb usage too, he is also concerned with a notional as opposed to a structural presentation of language in use. The notional approach Herbert employs is concerned with the way in which structurally different sentences can be used to express notionally identical statements. His notions include the expression of quantity, velocity, movement, dependence, purpose, etc. For example the notion of classification can be realised in the following ways.

There are	two three several many	*types kinds sorts classes varieties*	of bearings.	
Bearings are	*of* two, etc.	*types*, etc.	(*of* = belonging to).	
We can *classify*	bearings	according to	their position on the shaft. whether they take the load on the shaft or the end thrust.	
We can *divide*	bearings	into several	*classes categories groups*	according to ... (as above).

Although Herbert indicates the variety of structures which can be used to express a single concept, he gives little or no indication of when or under what circumstances it is more appropriate to use one rather than another. The impression may be given that these alternative realisations are simply stylistic variants of one another and their selection a matter of personal preference. It is more likely that the use of one rather than another is stringently controlled by the relative importance, as perceived by the writer, of the information he is presenting. Moreover, Herbert tends to confuse concepts that belong to science as a discipline and 'concepts' that belong to the communication of science as a subject. Thus velocity is a scientific concept whereas purpose and classification are communicative 'concepts' or acts. Quantity, movement, dependence, etc. have no particular status but are notional or semantic categories which may be realised by particular linguistic forms. However, Herbert's approach does represent an attempt to pedagogically organise features of the use of language in science and technology:

> 'Reading passages are specially written to illustrate selected features of technical style . . . Herbert stresses that he has tried to describe the technical statement (i.e. the complete sentence) rather than the individual word. Nevertheless, the emphasis is on . . . the systematic practice of relevant structures, and pointing out how the difficulty of technical vocabulary lies in the semi-scientific or semi-technical words which have a range of meaning and are frequently used idiomatically (e.g. work, load, force), and in the rather formal words which are partly responsible for what he described as "the slightly fossilised appearance of the typical scientific statement".' (Macmillan, 1971.)

3.3 *Current Perspectives*

Over the last five years or so views on the design of EST materials have increasingly taken into account both the learners specific purpose for learning the language, and a description of the language to be learnt that emphasises its character as communication as well as its formal properties. This concern with the communicative properties of language reflects an increasing interest in language functions both by linguistics and by language teachers. It is recognised that communicative competence consists of both the ability to handle the formal devices of the language which enable a user to create and combine sentences, and the ability 'to recognise how sentences are used in the performance of acts of communication, the ability to understand the rhetorical functioning of language in use'. (Allen and Widdowson, 1974: see Chapter 3.) Considered as communication, language ceases to be a separate subject, but becomes 'an aspect of other subjects' (ibid). Language as used in science is associated with the means that are characteristically employed in science to *reason*. Thus, the reasoning processes associated with defining, classifying, generalising from observation, drawing conclusions and so on, represent general communicative uses of language in science. Such acts of communication are part of presenting the 'content' of science.

Many of the papers in this book are written with this perspective in mind. These methodological features, or acts of communication, are incorporated into language learning materials for EST, both as the organising framework for course design of which the materials form a part, and quite explicitly in exercises that attempt to teach use – to practise the stating of definitions, classifications, explanations, observations, conclusions and so on. Such terms become a communicative metalanguage to refocus traditional grammatical terminology.

The move towards teaching communication in EST has coincided with a renewed interest in discourse analysis. Analyses of scientific writing in the past have tended to focus attention on the incidence of formal features such as the passive, relative clauses and the universal present together with specialist, vocabulary (see 3.2 above). Such descriptions, however, were essentially quantitative, and did little to characterise scientific discourse as communication. Recent approaches have emphasised the functional aspect of language use the way different acts of communication combine to produce a coherent and continuous passage of prose. (Labov, 1970, Widdowson, 1973, Jones, 1974, Sinclair *et al.*, 1975.) The particular relevance for EST lies in the applicability of such descriptions to the development of reading and listening comprehension materials. An analysis or characterisation of a piece of discourse has implications for the way interpretation takes place. Thus, understanding inter-sentential relationships has become an important aspect of developing interpretive competence. In addition, insight into the nature of scientific discourse has led to a concern for the authenticity of the text material prepared for learners. It is widely accepted that learners should be presented with learning material that is both authentic – appropriate as communication and simplified – appropriate to their level. Simplification strategies applied to textual material need not necessarily result in inauthentic discourse, particularly when such material is composed rather than adapted (see Chapter 3).

A view of language as communication has had a profound influence on the direction of ESP over the last few years. Both the language to be taught and the purpose of teaching it have, as it were, come into focus much more closely as a consequence of the notion. It has enabled the writing of teaching materials to escape the narrow framework of structuralist linguistics, to be concerned with 'how the total system operates to convey meanings and messages,' as Candlin puts it in Chapter 10. English for Special Purposes, and EST in particular, is rapidly becoming as a result, not just a major growth field within general ELT, but the dominant approach to the teaching of English as a Foreign Language.

REFERENCES

Allen, J. P. B. and Widdowson, H. G., 'Teaching the Communicative Use of English' in *I.R.A.L.*, XII/1, February, 1974, reprinted in this volume as Chapter 3.

Allen, J. P. B. and Widdowson, H. G., *English in Physical Science*, OUP, 1974.

Ewer, J. R. and Lattore, G., 'Preparing an English course for Students of Science' in *English Language Teaching*, Vol. XXI, No. 3, 1967.

Ewer, J. R., 'Further notes on Developing an English programme for students of Science and Technology' in *English Language Teaching*, Vol. XXVI, No. 1, 1971 and Vol. XXVI, No. 3, 1972.

Herbert, A. J., *The Structure of Technical English*, Longman, 1965.

Jones, K., 'The Role of Discourse Analysis in Devising Undergraduate Reading Programmes in EST', ETIC mimeo, 1974.

Jordan, R. R. and Mackay, R., 'A Survey of the Spoken English Problems of Overseas Postgraduates at the Universities of Manchester and Newcastle,' in *Journal of the Institute of Education*, Newcastle, 1973.

Labov, W., 'The Study of Language in its Social Context' in *Studium Generale*, Vol. 23, 1970, reproduced in Giglioli, P. P. (ed.) *Language and Social Context*, Penguin, 1972.

Macmillan, M., 'A Survey of Textbooks for EST' in *Science and Technology in a Second Language*, CILT Reports and Papers No. 7, CILT, London, 1971.

Perren, G., Foreword in *Teaching Languages to Adults for Special Purposes*. CILT Reports and Papers No. 11, CILT, London, 1974.

Sinclair, J. McH. and Coulthard, R. M., *Towards an Analysis of Discourse*, OUP, 1975.

Widdowson, H. G., *An Applied Linguistic Approach to Discourse Analysis*, University of Edinburgh, unpublished Ph.D. Thesis, 1973.

Widdowson, H. G., 'An approach to the Teaching of Scientific English Discourse' in *RELC Journal*, Vol. 5, No. 1, 1974.

Widdowson, H. G., 'EST in Theory and Practice' in *English for Academic Study*, ETIC, April, 1975.

2

Identifying the Nature of the Learner's Needs

R. MACKAY

Learners of English as an auxiliary to academic or professional skills are generally more aware of what they want to use English for.

In order to design and teach effective courses, the teacher and planner must investigate the uses to which the language will be put. Informal approaches to learners or their instructors in whatever professional field of study or vocational field they belong to will invariably lead to vague, confused and even erroneous results.

One of the reasons for this is that few non-linguistically trained people use language terminology rigorously or even in the same way to mean the same things. The linguistically unsophisticated confuse and conflate skills, or simply do not distinguish between them at all. They frequently underestimate the amount of knowledge of the foreign language needed to perform a given task. They almost always underestimate the time and effort involved in gaining a mastery of the language capable of permitting them to do whatever it is they want to do with it.

Hence, it is the responsibility of these language teachers involved in planning courses for given groups of learners for specific purposes, to determine accurately what these specific purposes are. Then the teacher is one step nearer being able to translate these needs into linguistic and pedagogic terms in order to produce and teach an effective course. There are basically two formal ways of gathering the necessary information: by a questionnaire to be completed by the learner or teacher, or by means of a structured interview.

If a questionnaire is to be used, the teacher must determine what kind of information about what he requires and design questions to elicit this information. It is very important that the specific points upon which the information is required be determined before the questionnaire is made up. This will ensure that all the areas upon which information is required will be covered. Those and no more. Asking as many questions as possible, and then settling down to

21

extract relevant information from the results, is uneconomic and time wasting for both the provider of the information and the gatherer. Moreover it frequently results in serious gaps in the resulting information. Re-runs are costly and tedious to carry out. Hence the correct questions and the appropriate number of questions must be asked on the first full run.

A pilot run with the first version of the questionnaire is a good idea. Even administered on a few, say five, individuals, it will indicate what questions have been poorly or ambiguously phrased and if any important information is missing.

A structured interview is similar in format construction and purpose to a questionnaire. Its difference lies in that it is not completed by the person providing the information, but is completed by the gatherer of the information who asks the questions contained on the interview sheet directly of the individual whose needs are being investigated.

The structured interview has several advantages over the questionnaire. Firstly, since the gatherer is asking the questions, none of them will be left unanswered as frequently happens in question-naires.

Secondly, the gatherer can clarify any misunderstanding which may crop up in the interpretation of the questions. Thirdly and perhaps most advantageously, the gatherer can follow up any avenue of interest which arises during the question and answer session but which had not been forseen during the designing of the structured interview.

1 Interview conducted at the National Autonomous University of Mexico

The following structured interviews were used in a basic information gathering project conducted by the Research and Development Unit (English Language) of the National Autonomous University of Mexico prior to designing a special purpose English Language course for undergraduates in the Faculty of Veterinary Medicine.

In order to be as thorough as possible, we decided to administer two sets of structured interviews – one to the teaching staff and the other to the undergraduates whom they taught. In this way we would be able to identify any discrepancy between the needs as stated by the professors and those as stated by the student body.

First of all, the professor's interview.

We wanted the name of the faculty, the subject he taught and his own name, the latter in case we wished to return to him at some future date. The subject, to ensure that we interviewed professors from all subjects taught in the faculty. We in no way wished to bias the answers given. Hence we began by ascertaining what percentage of required reading was in fact available in *Spanish*. Then we asked Q. No. 2 which still does not mention English. In fact, the only *question* involving English is the last one Q. No. 8! Q. No. 3 and 4 were included to find out about the necessity or otherwise for familiarity with a foreign language in order first to pass the subject concerned and secondly to graduate in that field.

Q. No. 6 was included to provide us with a crosscheck for any anomalous answer to Q. No. 5. Presumably, if graduate work were conducted abroad, it would be done in one of the countries which excelled in this field. Moreover, the language of the country where postgraduate studies were carried out would most likely influence the choice of foreign language, if any, in which the professor read to prepare his classes.

Q. No. 7 sought to identify the nature of the reading material recommended to undergraduates e.g. textbooks, scientific papers, journals, etc., it would also provide us with references permitting us to examine these for characteristics of style, lexis, etc. and provide us with a potential source of relevant material from which teaching texts could be extracted.

The last Q, Q. No. 8, asks directly for the professor's opinion as to the usefulness of English not to pass the course or to graduate (Q.'s 3 and 4) but to graduate as *well qualified* professionals.

Our guess had been that English or any other foreign language was not, in fact, necessary for undergraduates either to pass their courses or to graduate. If this were the case (and it proved to be so) then we wanted to know if English were *at all* important in that faculty.

There exists the danger that because foreign language teachers make their livings from teaching foreign languages, they exaggerate the importance of and the need for their particular language for given groups of learners. This results in frustration for both the teachers and the students. The students end up struggling with a foreign language for which the vast majority have no need; the teachers find themselves teaching, usually unsuccessfully, unwilling and uncooperative students. This situation occurs all too frequently. We wanted to avoid it in the National Autonomous University of Mexico.

The student's version of the structured interview follows a similar pattern to the professor's version.

Most of the information could be checked directly one against the other to determine whether there was substantial disagreement, on any point, between the two groups.

Again, we were avoiding the accusation of biasing the interview in favour of English – Q. No. 2 gives us the two most important foreign languages, *whether or not* English is one of them.

Q. No. 5 checked, against students who did claim to read in a foreign language, how frequently they actually did so, what type of material and with what facility.

It also elicited information on the usefulness of a foreign language, and the specific language(s) that those who only read in Spanish need.

It also elicited, from those who only read in Spanish, information as to whether they thought they were missing something or not.

The sample of vet-school undergraduates was selected by catching students learning lectures on each subject until a student for each subject from each semester of the entire vet. course had been interviewed. So, it can be seen that besides being an essential first step in planning EST courses, basic information gathering must be conducted thoroughly, honestly and only after a considerable amount of thought about what kind of information is going to be valuable.

The analysis and interpretation of the results of this set of structured interviews was reported on at the 2nd Annual MEXTESOL Convention in Mexico in October 1975 and published in the 'Working Papers' of the Unidad de Investigacion y Desarrollo (Lengua Inglesa) del CELE, UNAM, Mexico 20, D. F., December 1975.

STRUCTURED INTERVIEW · Ref. ID/basic Info/75

Professor's Version

Faculty
Subject
Professor's name

1 What proportion of the required reading for this course is available in Spanish?
None ☐ 0–24% ☐ 25–49% ☐ 50–74% ☐ 75% or more ☐

2 Are texts in a language other than Spanish recommended reading material for this course?

Yes ☐   No ☐

(If YES:

In what language(s) is the recommended reading material published?

most important_____

2nd most important_____)

3 In your opinion, is it *necessary* for your students to know a foreign language in order to pass this course?

Yes ☐   No ☐

(If YES:

What language(s) is/are *necessary*? (in order of importance)
For what purpose(s)?)

4 Do you consider it necessary to know a foreign language in order to graduate in veterinary medicine?

Yes ☐   No ☐

(If YES:

What language(s) is/are necessary? (in order of importance))
(If NO:

Do you think that your students could gain any benefit from knowing a foreign language?

Yes ☐   No ☐)

(If YES:

What language(s)? (in order of importance)
What benefits could they get?)

5 Do you find it necessary to read in a foreign language/languages in order to prepare your classes in this subject?

Yes ☐   No ☐

(If YES:

What language(s)? (in order of importance)
How frequently do you read in that/those language(s)?
Daily ☐   Weekly ☐   Monthly ☐   Occasionally ☐
With what facility do you read in that language/those languages?
What do you read in order to prepare your classes?)

6 Have you done postgraduate work?

Yes ☐ No ☐

(If YES:
Where did you do it?/specify institution and country/

7 What do you recommend your students to read in this course?
Please specify:
Which of these do you consider indispensible for the student to
PASS this course?

8 How would you describe the usefulness of ENGLISH for
graduating as a well-qualified professional in this field?

Necessary ☐ Convenient ☐ Unnecessary ☐

STRUCTURED INTERVIEW   Ref. ID/Basic Info/75.
Student Version   Faculty
                                    Subject
Student's name: Professor in Charge

1 What proportion of the required reading in this course is available
in Spanish?

None ☐ 0–24% ☐ 25–49% ☐ 50–74% ☐ 75% or more ☐

2 Are texts in a language other than Spanish recommended reading
material in this course?

Yes ☐ No ☐

(In what language(s) is/are the recommended material published?
most important_____
2nd most important_____)

3 In your opinion, is it NECESSARY to know a foreign language(s)
in order to PASS this course?

Yes ☐ No ☐

(What language(s) is/are necessary?)

4 Do you consider it NECESSARY to know a foreign language in
order to GRADUATE in this field?

Yes ☐ No ☐

a) What language(s) is/are necessary? _____
(in order of importance)

b) Why is it/are they needed? _____

5 Can you read in a foreign language?

Yes ☐ No ☐

(If affirmative, a) In what language(s)?

b) How frequently do you read in that/these languages?

Daily ☐ Weekly ☐ Monthly ☐ Occasionally ☐

c) How do you read?   fluently ☐

little difficulty ☐

some difficulty ☐

great difficulty ☐

d) What do you read?   basic texts ☐

professional journals ☐

theses/dissertations ☐

other (please specify) ☐)

(If negative)

Would knowing a foreign language help you in your studies?

Yes ☐ No ☐)

(if affirmative, what language(s)?

Why?)

6 What texts does your professor recommend you read in this course?

Author _____ Title _____

Which of these do you consider of greatest help in your studies?

7 How would you describe the usefulness of ENGLISH for graduating as a well-qualified professional in this field?

Necessary ☐ Convenient ☐ Unnecessary ☐

2 Questionnaire for SEAMEO Countries.*

The purpose of this brief questionnaire is to identify, as accurately as possible, the nature, number and location of English Language teaching programmes which provide English for Special Purposes in the SEAMEO Countries.

* This questionnaire was prepared for the SEAMEO Regional English Language Centre by Ronald Mackay, visiting Senior Consultant and Milagros Ibe, Specialist in Evaluation, August 1974.

By ESP is meant the teaching of English not as an end in itself but as an essential means to a clearly identifiable goal. Most ESP programmes will be concerned with teaching English to students whose primary interest lies in some branch of science, applied science, agriculture, medicine, administration, commerce or technology. The needs of the students may be roughly divided into:

Academic needs, where English is required for further academic study e.g. medical students requiring English in order to understand lectures/read medical textbooks in English, science students requiring instruction in the writing of scientific English etc. ; and,

Job needs, where English is required in order to perform a particular practical job e.g. technicians requiring English in order to work on a project in which English is used.

WHERE APPLICABLE PLEASE TICK THUS $\sqrt{}$ IN BOX PROVIDED, WHERE A BROKEN LINE IS PROVIDED PLEASE WRITE ANSWER. *PLEASE ANSWER* ALL THE QUESTIONS, EXCEPT THOSE IN PARENTHESES WHICH MAY BE OMITTED IF NOT APPLICABLE.

Do NOT write in this Column

1 Does your institution run a course/courses which can be regarded as a course/courses in ESP?

Yes ☐ No ☐

EVEN IF YOUR ANSWER TO QUESTION 1 IS NO, PLEASE COMPLETE THE QUESTIONS 2–13 BEFORE RETURNING THE QUESTIONNAIRE.

2 Are the needs which these English courses meet principally academic needs or job needs?

Academic ☐ Job ☐

NEEDS
ACADEMIC NEEDS
3 What is the special field or fields of study of the students?

. . . .

Do NOT write in this Column

4 What is the medium of instruction in that special field?

....

5 What is the age range of the students?

....

6 Are the students in

Secondary education ☐

Undergraduate courses ☐

Postgraduate courses ☐

Other (Please specify) ☐

....

7 For what specific purposes do these students require English?

Understanding lecturers in their special field of study in English ☐

Taking part in oral tutorials in English ☐

Reading textbooks in their special field in English ☐

Writing answers to examination questions or reports ☐

Other purposes (Please specify) ☐

....

8 Are there national goals or policies which encourage English Language teaching programmes to include ESP courses?

Yes ☐   No ☐

9 (Please specify) ....

....

....

10 Are there institutional goals or policies which encourage English Language teaching programmes to include ESP courses?

Yes ☐   No ☐

11 (Please specify) . . . .
. . . .
. . . .

12 Is there any indication that ESP courses would be welcomed in your institution?

Yes ☐   No ☐

13 (Please specify) . . . .
. . . .
. . . .

JOB NEEDS

14 For what jobs or purposes is the student being trained?
. . . .

15 What is the age range of the students?
. . . .

16 Why do the students require English? Because

The main language of the job is English ☐

They are working with English-speaking colleagues ☐

Some/most/all of the written or printed materials connected with the job are in English ☐

They have to convey information or instructions from English Language sources to non-English speaking workers ☐

Some/most/all correspondence has to be conducted in English ☐

They have to follow training courses conducted in English ☐

Other (Please specify) ☐
. . . .

17 Do they require English for

Understanding ☐

Reading ☐

	Do NOT write in this Column

Speaking ☐

Writing ☐

Other purposes (Please specify) ☐

. . . .

THE COURSES

18 Are the ESP courses in your institution organised and run by

   (a) A central 'service' department e.g. a Language Centre?

                    Yes ☐ No ☐

   (b) The English Department?

                    Yes ☐ No ☐

   (c) Separate departments for their own students?

                    Yes ☐ No ☐

   (d) Others?

      (Please specify) . . . .

      . . . .

      . . . .

19 In what year/years of their studies do they receive English Language classes?

. . . .

20 Is attendance at these English classes obligatory?

                    Yes ☐ No ☐

21 How many hours of English instruction a week do they receive?

. . . .

22 How many weeks per year do the English classes last?

. . . .

23 Is there a final examination in English?

                    Yes ☐ No ☐

25 How many ESP courses does your institution run per year?

. . . .

26 How many teaching hours does each course last for?

. . . .

27 What is the total number of students per year who attend these courses?

. . . .

28 What is the approximate size of each class?

. . . .

29 Does your institution run different kinds of ESP courses catering for different needs?

Yes ☐ No ☐

30 (Please list the course or courses and describe the aims of each briefly.)

. . . .
. . . .
. . . .
. . . .
. . . .

31 How many years of English instruction have the students had before attending these courses?

. . . .

32 Do your courses cater for different levels of proficiency?

Yes ☐ No ☐

33 (If yes, describe briefly) . . . .
. . . .
. . . .

34 Are the students tested for proficiency in English before being admitted to the ESP courses?

Yes ☐ No ☐

35 Do you offer ESP instruction to complete beginners in English?

Yes ☐ No ☐

36 What proportion of the time spent teaching English on these courses involves *remedial instruction*? (i.e. re-teaching points which were already taught at school but inadequately learned.)

$\frac{1}{10}$ ☐ $\frac{1}{8}$ ☐ $\frac{1}{5}$ ☐ $\frac{1}{4}$ ☐ $\frac{1}{3}$ ☐ $\frac{1}{2}$ ☐

(If more, please state.)

. . . .

37 What proportion of the time on these courses is involved in the development of language skills (i.e. developing upon what the students have already learned?

$\frac{1}{10}$ ☐ $\frac{1}{8}$ ☐ $\frac{1}{5}$ ☐ $\frac{1}{4}$ ☐ $\frac{1}{3}$ ☐ $\frac{1}{2}$ ☐

(If more, please state.)

. . . .

38 By means of the numbers 1 (most), 2, 3, and 4 (least) indicate the time the course devotes to each skill.

Listening . . . .
Speaking . . . .
Reading . . . .
Writing . . . .

39 Are there any of these skills which are ignored as not being relevant to the students' needs?

Yes ☐   No ☐

40 (If so, which?)

Listening ☐
Speaking ☐
Reading ☐
Writing ☐

41 What proportion of the ESP course time is spent in

Classroom teaching . . . .
Language laboratory . . . .
Others (Please specify) . . . .

. . . .

42 Do you use a tape-recorder as a teaching aid?
    Yes ☐   No ☐

43 (For what purpose?) ....
    ....

MATERIALS

44 Are published textbooks used on these courses?
    Yes ☐   No ☐

45 (Give the title, author's name and publisher of each of these textbooks.)
    ....
    ....
    ....

46 Are published materials used in the language laboratory?
    Yes ☐   No ☐

47 (Give the title, author's name and publisher of each of such tape courses.)
    ....
    ....
    ....

48 Are teaching materials specially prepared in your institution?
    Yes ☐   No ☐

49 Do they cover the needs of the entire course?
    Yes ☐   No ☐

50 Are there supplementary materials?
    Yes ☐   No ☐

51 (Describe briefly the purpose and content of the materials.)
    ....
    ....
    ....
    ....

Do NOT write in this Column

52 Who prepared them?........................
....

53 Can you make a sample copy available to RELC?
Yes ☐   No ☐

RESEARCH AND DEVELOPMENT

54 Is there any ESP materials writing project going on in your institution?
Yes ☐   No ☐

55 (Describe it. Name those involved/hours per week/aims.)
....
....
....
....

56 Is a progress report available?
Yes ☐   No ☐

57 Are there any other materials used in your ESP courses which have not been mentioned?
Yes ☐   No ☐

58 (Please specify, e.g. films) ....
....
....

59 Is there any ESP research project going on in your institution?
Yes ☐   No ☐

60 (Describe it, Name those involved/hours per week/aims.)
....
....
....

61 Is a progress report available?
Yes ☐   No ☐

Do NOT
write in
this Column

THE TEACHERS

62 How many teachers/lecturers are involved in ESP courses in your situation?
Full time ....
Part time ....

63 Do the part-time teachers have other and primary duties *within* your institution?
All of them ☐
Most of them ☐
Some of them ☐
None of them ☐

64 How may hours per week does each teacher teach on these courses?
Full time ....
Part time ....

65 Have they any other official duties in
Your own institution ☐
Other institutions ☐

66 (Please specify) ....
....
....

67 Do the ESP teachers work in collaboration with the subject teachers/lecturers, e.g. the lecturers in science or the special field of study of the students?
Yes ☐ No ☐

68 (What kind of cooperation is involved?)
....
....

69 Have the teachers any special training or instruction before being required to teach these ESP courses?
Yes ☐ No ☐

Do NOT write in this Column

70 (Please specify) ....

....

....

71 Are there any native speakers of English employed in these ESP courses?

Yes ☐   No ☐

72 (Please name them) ....

....

....

73 (Name the sponsoring body) ....

....

74 Is there any other information you feel is relevant to the aims of this questionnaire?

Yes ☐   No ☐

75 (Please specify) ....

....

....

....

PART TWO

Approaches to ESP Textbook Design

In Part I we identified some of the factors that characterise ESP. We discussed some of the theoretical implications of an approach to ESP which emphasises the communicative properties of language. We also suggested practical ways of identifying learners' needs through an interview or by means of a questionnaire. The papers in Part II describe the thinking behind the writing of three textbooks published in recent years which attempt to provide teachers and learners with relevant material for EST courses.* These materials represent a generalised solution to the problems posed by EST learning situations, although both *Writing Scientific English* and *Nucleus* were originally written to service the needs of a specific group of learners in the Universities of Libya and Tabriz. In Part III we shall concern ourselves with Case Studies of more particular responses to specific situations.

The three textbooks have certain basic features in common, which may be summarised as follows:

1 All three are aimed at students who are in their first year of tertiary level education.
2 All three presuppose that learners have had a considerable amount of English tuition at the Secondary level and possess, what might be called 'a dormant competence' in English.
3 All three share the view that the difficulties which students have appear to arise from their unfamiliarity with English use in scientific writing.
4 All three take an approach to the selection and grading of linguistic items to be practised which emphasises the communicative function as well as, and in relation to, linguistic forms.

* Swales, J., *Writing Scientific English*, Nelson, 1971.
  English in Focus: English in Phsical Science, Allen, J. P. B. and Widdowson, H. G., OUP, 1974.
  Nucleus: General Science, Bates, M. and Dudley-Evans, A., Longman, 1976.

5 All three make the assumption that learners have acquired a knowledge of basic science during their Secondary level education.

Of course, there are considerable differences in scope and methodology in the textbooks themselves, which it is not our purpose to evaluate, but this should not be allowed to mask the considerable similarities of intention and approach.

Swales gives a detailed account of exactly how the decision to prepare a course to teach scientific writing to engineering students was arrived at. After ranking students needs at the University in 'decreasing order of importance as Reading, Listening, Writing and Speaking', Swales makes the observation that 'it has usually been taken for granted that such skill priorities should be directly reflected in a properly established ESP programme'. He goes on, however, to point out that

> 'it does not necessarily follow from the fact that reading has been identified as being the greatest need that it should be assigned the largest proportion of language time. It does not follow because it is equally important to consider what the language teacher can most usefully do in the limited time available to him. In other words, decisions about course priorities should be partly based on an assessment of the circumstances under which teacher intervention in the learning process is essential, where it is useful, and where it is of marginal advantage.'

We consider this point of view of very considerable practical significance. As a consequence Swales and his colleagues decided to focus attention largely on productive writing skills where their 'role (as teachers and materials writers) was so much clearer'. This accounts for the title, and content, of the textbook as *Writing Scientific English*. It also emphasises the difference between a course book such as 'English in Physical Science' written as an applied linguistic contribution, but *outside* a specific learning situation and one written as a result of having to cater for a particular group of learners in a particular learning and teaching environment.

The paper by Allen and Widdowson introduces certain distinctions that we have referred to in Chapter 1 and which now form part of the basic metalanguage of EST; the distinctions between use and usage, the rhetorical coherence of discourse and the grammatical cohesion of text. These distinctions are clearly exemplified in the exercises that are quoted and discussed in the paper. A feature of the approach Allen and Widdowson are describing is the close relationship that is established between the development of receptive reading and productive writing skills. Comprehension and composition are seen as twin aspects of the skill of interpretation. By interpretation we mean the ability to process and pattern data – key skills at this level of education in Science. Learners are first given practice in perceiving how certain communicative acts can be made explicit, and how relationships in texts are established and maintained. Then learners are required to perform such acts for themselves, which eventually leads to paragraph writing in which the learners are required to build up a text, to manipulate sentence structure and relationships. At each stage 'writing practice is based on the reading passage'. This is not done as a meaningless manipulation of sentence patterns but as a use of English in the performance of different communicative acts relevant to the learners special subject of study. Thus, writing practice facilitates reading comprehension, and vice versa.

The *Nucleus* materials appear to represent a similar response, in which oral/aural skills are focussed upon strongly in a situation where the development of reading skills would seem to be prior. But, as Martin Bates points out, in the situation he and the team were in, there were considerable problems 'involved in investigating the English language reading and aural learning needs of the students. Not only were there the usual variations in language use depending on subject level and medium; there was also considerable extra stylistic diversity including features of Indian Spoken English and Russian Written English. These problems were aggravated by the fact that our Service English Courses were given in the first and second years, whereas most students did not experience a really urgent need for English until the latter part of the course.' As a consequence, the writers of *Nucleus* decided that 'at the early stages there should be plenty of active use of English, encouraging students to participate, giving them confidence and a feel for the communicative value of the language which would lead into *passive* reading and listening exercises (at later stages of the Course).'

An important part of Bates's paper concerns the decision to adopt a functional/notional approach to syllabus design rather than structural/frequency count approach. 'We felt the need,' he says, 'to teach the communicative value and situational use of language rather than paradigms of language forms in isolation from context.' He shows how the arrangement of concepts and associated language forms facilitated the development of a 'cyclical' course with a cumulative learning effect. In addition,

'Concepts formed a bridge between the scientific knowledge and the rhetorical resources by means of which this knowledge could be organised and communicated in the foreign language.'

But the main advantage of using concepts as the basis for selecting language forms was that

'they encouraged language *transfer* and enabled the student to apply what he had learned to different contexts – linguistic, situational and functional. They were not tied to any particular unit of language whether lexical, situational or rhetorical.'

Thus, *causation* can embrace causitive verbs, clause types and logical connection. The concept of *structure* can be applied equally to the cell or the atom; concepts such as *property*, *measurement* and *function* are germane to the making of *definitions*, *descriptions*, *explanations* etc.

The *Nucleus* team are sharply aware of the need for specialist advice on the planning and ordering of the content of any science-oriented course. Moreover, the need for appropriate preparation for teachers about to embark on the teaching of special-purpose courses is evident. When the methodological aspects of science teaching are taken up and exploited by English language teachers (see Chapter 1, 3.3), the possibilities of teaching inappropriate language and/or incorrect science arise. In such circumstances, the science informant is invaluable as a guide, critic and source of data.

One final point: Bates frequently draws attention to the compromises involved in designing *Nucleus*. Compromises – 'academic, linguistic, pedagogic, geographic, personal' – operate at all levels of design. The reconciliation of different linguistic and extralinguistic viewpoints and situational demands we see as integral to the professional role of the EST practitioner, and an essential aspect of any language teaching operation.

3

Writing
'Writing Scientific English'

JOHN SWALES

1

The book *Writing Scientific English* (WSE) reached a form almost
identical to that in which it was eventually published in the winter and
spring of 1969/70 during my last year as Head of the English
Department, Faculty of Engineering, University of Libya. In most
respects WSE was a third response to the following situation. The
faculties of Agriculture, Engineering and Science were English-
medium and had been established in the early sixties; the majority of
students who entered the University came from Arabic-medium
secondary schools roughly modelled on the Egyptian pattern. Such
schools were broad-curriculum and placed a strong emphasis on
factual information and terminological accuracy, much of which
acquired by rote-learning. In many ways, therefore, Libyan
Secondary schools tended to perpetuate the verbalistic tradition in
Middle East education and, for all their virtues, provided very little
training in the application of scientific experimental method. For this
reason, the first two years of the five-year Engineering degree course
were devoted to something very like an 'A-Level' course in Physics,
Chemistry and Maths with additional subjects such as Workshop
Technology, Engineering Drawing and Strength of Materials. This in
turn meant that contact hours were as high as 30 per week, of which
five hours in the First Year and three in the Second were allotted to
English. The students had studied English at school for about six
hours a week for six years and had, on university entry, the expected
EFL post-secondary strengths and weaknesses – reasonable
vocabulary, grammatical 'knowledge', and graphology, the basis of a
servicable written and aural comprehension, serious interference
problems, both linguistic and cultural, in their free written work, and
quite understandable inhibitions about speaking English.

During my four years at Tripoli there were usually five members of
the English Department and, as I come increasingly to believe that

the teacher-variable is of great importance in ESP work[1], I think that it is worth summarising the strengths and weaknesses of this team. Only one member, James Cormick, had a scientific background, and nobody had any professional knowledge of curriculum development, behavioural educational objectives, or tertiary-level study skills. Hugh Mildmay and I were the only ones who had taken an ELT/Linguistics course. However, on the more positive side, a majority of the English staff could usually claim to have had previous experience of teaching English in the Arab world and to have at least some acquaintance with the Arabic language. This experience, I would like to believe, led to a certain sympathy with the students and to some understanding of their linguistic difficulties, and perhaps this concern to avoid taking aspects of Technical English usage for granted is reflected in the better parts of WSE. We were at least semi-consciously aware that our students came from a strong but very different culture to that of western Europe, with its own conventions about methods of study and teaching and with its own conventions about formal writing.

However, there were a number of reasons why it took so long to translate this grasp of what might be needed into sets of passable teaching materials. In the first place, when I arrived in Tripoli in 1966 we had very little information about the characteristics of Scientific English. I managed to get a photo-copy of Barber's article[2], there were one or two fairly useful articles in the ELT Journal, and Herbert's textbook[3] had recently appeared, but, unlike people entering the EST field today, we had to start the surveys of textbooks, lab reports and technical manuals pretty well from scratch. This meant that it was almost two years before I felt I knew enough about the use of the Verb in the Science and Engineering materials used by our students to move on to other areas. Secondly, the mid-sixties were a time of great advance in the study of English syntax, and it seemed in particular that Transformational Grammar and the Grammar principally associated with M. A. K. Halliday were going to be tools of immense and direct benefit in the preparation of ELT materials. The partial and restricted practical value of frequency counts and sentence analyses had not yet become apparent, and 'the fallacy of the excluded functional middle' had yet to be demonstrated. Our low level of self-confidence in the face of these dramatic developments in syntactic theory made us feel that when we discovered that our statistical tables and transformational analyses were not necessarily leading to better courses this was because we had still not got enough *linguistic* information. Thirdly, interests in syntactic theory, in the special features of scientific and technical English, and in Arabic–English contrastive analysis kept me long over-concerned with classroom presentation and too long indifferent to ways of generating and simulating realistic language response and use in the class.

2

The courses we gave at the University of Libya concentrated on the productive skills; writing in the classroom and speaking in the Language Lab.[4] This is a decision that has come under criticism, has remained controversial and was, I believe, reversed some time after I left the Faculty of Engineering.[5] However, I am still inclined to think that the decision was right for the English Department then, and may well be right for an English Department in a similar position now.

Our experience of the learning environment showed that the students were mainly concerned in their course-work with studying their science textbooks, reading lecture notes and hand-outs, listening to lectures, and carrying out instructions – which might be in Arabic – in the laboratories and workshops. Their main writing tasks were taking notes from lectures, writing reports of various kinds and writing examination answers, many of these activities requiring, of course, numerate and graphic skills as well. Therefore, the students' needs in terms of the traditional language skills could be ranked in decreasing order of importance as Reading, Listening, Writing and Speaking. Now, it has usually been taken for granted that such skill priorities should be directly reflected in a properly-established ESP programme. It seems to me, however, that it does not necessarily follow from the fact that reading has been identified as being the greatest need that it should be assigned the largest proportion of language time. It does not follow because it is equally important to consider what the language teacher can most usefully do in the limited time available to him. In other words, decisions about course priorities should be partly based on an assessment of the circumstances under which teacher intervention in the learning process is essential, where it is useful and where it is of marginal advantage.

A quick review of the Tripoli situation showed that we were dealing with concurrent Science and English courses, that contact hours were high and students worked hard. We could expect then that students would spend at least 15 hours a week listening to science and maths lectures, would have further exposure to listening and reading in the labs and workshops, and would spend at least 12 hours a week on private study, some of it in the memorisation of laws, formulae and factual data. I therefore decided that the receptive reading and listening skills would have to largely look after themselves, the only regular exception being that we did spend time on a variety of 'Visualisation' exercises, of which Exercise 19(a) on page 113 of WSE has mysteriously survived.

The situation in the Faculty of Engineering was, however, unusual in terms of the relatively restricted reading programme it required of its students, and there is no doubt that in the neighbouring Faculty of Science the students of Botany, Biology and Zoology were faced with reading tasks of a different order of magnitude. The situation was, by contrast, typical in that we, as English teachers, had little idea about the *teaching* rather than the *testing* of reading. If I had understood the science texts better myself and had seen more clearly how passages from them might be profitably used in English classes, if I had known then what little I know now about the teaching of study-skills, or if we had had no language laboratory, I might have been persuaded to come to a different conclusion. The conclusion I did come to was, I still feel, a reasonable one given the general circumstances.

Our role, after all, was so much clearer on the 'productive' side. On entry, student writing was demonstrably very poor, as was their capacity to express themselves in speech. There were questions set in the examinations such as 'Describe the A.C. Dynamo' or 'Define stress, strain and elastic limit' for which the students had little guided preparation in their science courses, and their lab. and workshop reports were not often corrected for language and lay-out by their engineering lecturers. Thirdly, a writing/speaking orientation would allow us to keep rather more within our scientific depth. Fourthly, the more confidence we could give the students in their writing ability, the less likely they would be to fall back on the educationally unsatisfactory procedure of learning paragraphs and pages from their textbooks by heart. Fifthly, we had a good enough staff-student ratio to be able to correct the students' work, and we could use the lab. for remedial work on the recurrent grammatical errors. And in the end we knew that even spending about 130 hours over two years on a writing course would still not bring very many students to an ability level in written scientific English that might be expected of 'A-Level' Physics candidates.

3

In the last section I tried to outline those aspects of the educational situation at the University of Libya which, in hindsight, appeared to have particular influence on the ways in which we attempted to develop our courses to suit our students needs and interests, and to show that, by and large, our response was pragmatic and local. However, I have already mentioned a susceptibility at that time to Linguistic developments and, regrettably, some of these worked their way into the 69/70 materials in a rather obtrusive manner and were not subjected to the same standard of class-testing as the rest of the course. Examples of these exceptions to the general pragmatism are the incorporation of Boyd and Thorne's[6] distinction between the illocutionary forces of statements and predictions in the section on Modals (p. 35), the formulaic aspects of the Nominalisation section of Unit 10, which derive in large part from Lees's[7] book on the subject, and the inclusion of the rather unuseful section on Naming and the Possessive Genitive from the same Unit. This last came out of a small piece of research that I did in 1969, and the main findings found their way into WSE for what I now recognise as self-indulgent reasons. Otherwise, the main features of the book grew out of and took shape from our class-room experience. Two of these features are worth commenting on. First, WSE is fairly explicit about language forms and functions; secondly, the Units are not standardised in any way other than for approximate length.

The book is 'heavy' on explanations for several reasons. One is that we came to recognise that science and engineering students are used to coping with generalised concepts, technical expositions and symbolic representations. We therefore saw, and eventually found, no good reasons for not trying to utilise this capacity for abstract thinking, and for not trying at the same time to enhance the subject of English in the students' eyes by making it appear somewhat technical. In addition, we found in practice that there were occasions when the need for teacher-talk about Scientific English arose quite naturally in class and that our off-the-cuff efforts could always be improved upon in retrospect. WSE may not have got the balance between practice and percept right, but that both elements should be given attention I grew not to doubt.

WSE contains three main types of explanatory material. First, there are what might be called *Communication Frames*. Here, for example, is the opening paragraph from the Unit on Tables and Graphs (p. 146):

> Tables and graphs occur frequently in many kinds of scientific and technical writing because they display information in a clear and concise way. However, the information contained in such tables and graphs also usually requires a certain amount of written explanation and discussion. Of course, the written work should not merely describe in detail all the information contained in the table. This would be pointless. In fact, the writer usually wants to pick out the most significant information. He may want to contrast one set of figures with another set, or he may want to compare his results with someone else's.

Such scene-setting remarks were primarily designed to alter student attitudes. In earlier drafts we often found that the students lapsed in concentration when they felt that they had already 'done' the language points being practised. In later drafts we tried to counteract this by emphasising that accuracy with language would not itself necessarily lead to successful communication; what was 'new' – and indeed difficult for students with an Arabic-language background – was to learn to identify suitable places in a piece of written English for various kinds of statement. We hoped, especially in the second year, to develop an appreciation of the over-all context and purpose of the writing task before the task was attempted.

Secondly, there are a considerable number of *Usage Explanations*, such as why, where and how the Passive is used in Scientific English. Here is a slightly less stereotyped example from Unit 5 (p. 55):

> Relative clauses are used to avoid writing a series of very short sentences. They also enable the writer to keep the most important information for the main clause and to use relative clauses for the less important information. The main clause generally describes the result or demonstrates the principle. The relative clause generally describes conditions and circumstances.

Although we grew to feel that the students needed to be shown why they were being recommended to go about certain writing tasks in certain ways, we were certainly not always able to satisfy these needs. The struggles that both staff and students went through in an attempt to come to grips with the use of the commoner Modal verbs in Scientific English is a case in point. We produced a long chapter on Modals for the 68/69 course, but it was a clear failure as far as actual English classes were concerned. I then had a look at the use of Modals in the First and Third Year 1969 Technology exam scripts and this showed that the Third Year, who had had no instruction in English for the previous nine months, had managed to use the commoner Modal verbs very much better than the First Year had done. Our sense of failure was therefore corroborated. Rather more diffidently I also concluded that the use of *may, might, would,* etc. was an aspect of English that most of our students could only pick up as their feel for Scientific and Technical language developed through prolonged exposure. (The forms, both active and passive, could be taught easily enough but this did not take anybody very far.) Therefore, when I came to put WSE together my original intention was to omit all reference to Modals as a separate topic, but the strength of this conviction eventually ebbed away and the three pages tacked on to the end of Unit 3 is the unsatisfactory compromise. A similar story lies behind the Relative Clause 'Explanation' quoted above. There was no doubt that many of our students needed not only work on *how* to relativise, but also needed help on when to do so. The final outcome on page 55 was probably not the worst of several bad jobs, but I am still nervous about its linguistic validity.

Thirdly, there were *Language Displays*, some of which made use of a crude form of TG notation, such as the following:

(art) + Nominal + *wh*-word + BE + *not* + Verb-*ed* + ∅
   the   liquid   which   was   not   wanted
(art) + UN + verb-*ed* + Nominal
   the   unwanted   liquid

As I have already intimated, we found that there was little point in simplifying the information about language forms because many students so obviously responded favourably to a 'technical treatment' of English grammar – they felt that such a treatment was appropriate to their new status as Engineering students.

I have thus tried to explain how it came about that WSE is more of a 'grammar book' than most EST courses before or since. The other main way in which WSE diverges from its competitors is that it does not provide a set pattern of work. Apart from the fact that the Units have been kept to roughly the same length (in fact the number of exercises varies from 14 to 20), in every other way each Unit was allowed to develop in the direction that seemed to best suit its main teaching points. The number of sections in a Unit varies from two to six, and some Units such as those on Dimensions and Comparisons contain quite a lot of work based on non-verbal information, others such as those dealing with Definitions and More Concise Statements have none. The variations in the types of exercise follow two parameters, one being whether the required outputs are series of single sentences or passages. The other is whether the exercise is essentially manipulative (*Grammar*), whether it requires in addition decisions about style and organisation and/or selection from a largely given content (*Grammar Plus*), or whether the exercise is relatively free in that it requires the student to supply a good part of the content (*Open*). 120 of the 196 exercises in the book are single-sentence and 76 are passage exercises, the number of the latter varying from 2 in the Relative Clause Unit to 15 in the first Unit on Descriptions. Although the passage exercises become a majority in some of the later Units, they are spread fairly generally throughout the course, there being 5, for instance, in the first Unit. In total, there are 49 Grammar exercises, 74 Grammar Plus, and 73 Open exercises. In a few of the later Units there are no Grammar exercises at all, the Grammar Plus exercises occur in varying numbers in all Units, the extremes being 3 in Unit 2 and 12 in Unit 8, and the Open exercises also vary in numbers from 2 in Unit 5 to 9 in Unit 6.

Although the exercises that required little more than performing a grammatical 'trick' were largely phased out after Unit 7, WSE is not, on the whole, a steeply-graded course. This, however, was not the original plan; in early drafts the first term materials were very simple because at that time we followed the accepted practice of restricting the freer Open exercises to the later stages. We soon learnt that this was a mistake. First of all, we had to acknowledge the fact that the teacher could only get reliable information about the writing abilities of his class by giving them a few suitable freer-writing tasks. Moreover, it became our feeling that the classes themselves felt a need to express scientific information, rather than play around with the re-expression of bits of it. After all, the students were following concurrent Science and English courses and, from their arrival, had been faced with English writing problems in their technical subjects – all the more reason then to give them practice in semi-sustained scientific communication under improved conditions (language preparation, an exercise modified by trials with previous classes, a teacher on hand to help, correction, model answers, etc.). As the students had, as it were, been thrown in at the deep end right from the beginning, I decided to switch to shallow over-all grading, but with steep grading in each Unit.

4

The Grammar exercises were relatively easy to write; the Open exercises were largely a matter of 'hit and hope'. No amount of thought and care in the preparation ever seemed to guarantee success and many had to be scrapped as unsuitable, the ones appearing in WSE being, for the most part, those that the classes either enjoyed or could generally cope with. It was the Grammar Plus exercises that presented the real challenge. We wanted to devise exercises that both presented the language that was needed and at the same time forced attention on the meaning and/or organisation of what was being written in response. In 1968 I came up with 'Matching Tables', of which the following is a part-illustration (p. 72):

> ... Join one sentence from the left-hand column and one from the right-hand column.
>
> Tungsten is a metal.   It contains acetic acid.
> Water is a liquid.   It contains a large proportion of copper.
> Vinegar is a liquid.   It retains hardness at red heat.
> Brass is an alloy.   It consists of two parts of hydrogen and one part of water.

In the end I included nine of these in WSE. Admittedly, they are very artificial and also rather uneconomical in terms of words written per minute. However, the students found them challenging and interesting, they were usually keenly and carefully done, they are excellent for pair-work discussion and they make their grammatical points with conviction. At about the same time we started to make use of illustrations and tables as forms of data on which exercises could be built. These exercises, several of which were devised by Hugh Mildmay, proved to be an effective way of compelling students to think about the role and place of general vis-a-vis particular statements. Sometimes, however, we found ourselves stuck for years with unimaginative and mechanical exercise-types. For instance, we always spent a little time early in the course on the structure of Negative statements and for three years we could do no better than the 'make-the following-sentences-negative' type of exercise. Finally I hit upon: 'If you think that certain of the following statements are not true, write them out as negative statements. If you think they are true, leave them' (p. 9).

Over all, my attitude was one of experimenting with as many different types of exercise as possible in the belief that no one type of exercise will work with all the students all the time. It never seemed to me that it was in any way necessary to deal with every topic in the same way irrespective of its nature, or that every exercise in a section should be just a little harder than the preceding one. If possible I preferred to work from a bank of exercises and explanations that I had had classroom experience of and then to fill in any obvious gaps as best I could, rather than to try and respond – possibly even less enterprisingly – to a cold syllabus statement.

5

The development (if that is the word) of the Unit on Definitions was fairly typical of the way the book came together and must suffice as an illustration of what tended to happen. As with a number of other key Units, there were basically four versions; course materials for 1967/68, 68/69 and 69/70 and the WSE version. The final draft of Definitions consists of four sections, which break down as follows:

  1 *Introduction* (9 sentences)
    – Communication Frame (why definitions are important)
    – Usage explanation (good and bad definitions)
    – Display of General Definition formula
    – Display of General Class Words + taxonomy exercise (ex 1)
  2 *General Definitions* (115 sentences)
    – Explanation + display of part of the formula
    – Matching Table of active and passive completions (ex 2)
    – Explanation of *device* + crossing-out exercise (ex 3)
    – Display of passive relative completions + open exercise (ex 4)
    – Open passive completion exercise + expansion exercise from notes (ex 5 & 6)
    – Display + open exercise on reduced instrumentals (ex 7)
    – Matching Table on active completions (ex 8)
    – Display of reduced actives + choice of *contain* and *consist of* (ex 9)
    – Display + exercise on prepositional relatives (ex 10)
    – Display of reductions to *with (the property of)* + exercise (ex 11)
    – Display of Complete formula + open defining exercise (ex 12)
  3 *Specific Definitions* (30 sentences)
    – Explanation of Use + display of the new formula
    – Controlled completion exercise (ex 13)
    – Open defining exercise (ex 14)

4 *Expanded Definitions* (25 2/3 sentence mini-paragraphs)
 – Display of Definition & Example
 – Completion exercise + open exercise (ex 15a and 15b)
 – Display of Definition & Use + completion exercise (ex 16)
 – Display of Definition & Main Parts + open exercise (ex 17)
 – Display of Expansions in summary form

Before looking at how and why the Definitions Unit came to take this shape, it will be necessary to make a brief comment on the changing purposes of the Unit and on the sources of information and ideas. In fact, the original intention was to use Definitions purely as a means of revising certain aspects of English grammar in a neat and economical way; in other words the *function* of definitions was not considered at all. The writing of definitions was to consolidate the following points; there is no definite article in general statements, the need for a copula verb, the difference between active and passive, and the main characteristics of English relative clauses, all of which caused problems for most Arab students. The second idea was that a definition offered a fairly automatic entry-mechanism to a student who had a writing task in front of him but who did not know how to start. It was not until the second draft that the predominating real function of definitions to introduce and circumscribe the main features of the topic became a little clearer and so became built into the embryonic Expanded Definitions section and into Units 8 and 9. The first approach to definitions was an unsystematic look at the form in which they occurred in Engineering hand-outs, and it was this that led to seizing on them for the purposes of grammatical revision. A more formal analysis of textbooks produced the General Definition Formula; a tape by James Cormick on prepositions plus relative markers led to what eventually became exercise 10; expanded definitions came largely from a study of technical dictionaries and encyclopaedias; an observation by David Barber in Benghazi regarding the fact that some definitions were ostensibly *about* the modifier was the start of Specific Definitions; and a later study of the use of definitions in science and engineering texts finally convinced me that I had not got enough insight into the reasons for the occurrence of definitions at places other than at the beginning of discourses to attempt more than a discourse-initial Communication Frame.

The 1967/68 course consisted of about half the exercise material of the final General Definition section (but with almost no supporting explanations) and a section on 'Nominal Definitions', e.g. 'The tool which tightens and loosens screws is called a screwdriver'. It was only much later that it dawned on me that this type of definition would never be needed by the students in their own writing; lecturers might well use them in their explanations, but if a student used a full Naming Statement in a report or an exam he would at best be thought to be behaving oddly by his superiors. The parts of the first draft that have survived are usually detectable because they are less technical, such as 'A shop is a place where things are bought and sold'. Originally too, students were asked to choose between *apparatus*, *instrument*, *machine* and *tool* as substitutes for *device*, but as neither staff or students could ever agree about this I later retreated to a crossing-out exercise (ex 3 in WSE). A similar thing happened to the attempt to deal with *contains*, *consists of* and *is composed of*, for this was another area that never got properly sorted out and in the end *is composed of* disappeared altogether simply because I could never make pedagogic sense with it. Ex 11 was the final old soldier who should have been dead and buried long before 1970, but who somehow never quite faded away.

The following year (68/69) saw a straightforward expansion of the first draft: Nominal definitions remained; the beginnings of the Definition formula and some explanatory material appeared, as did three pre-definition classification exercises, one I recollect as dealing with different sorts of containers in the Chemistry lab. There was also a start made on Expanded definitions in that students were asked for the first time to follow definitions with examples.

In the third draft the Introduction approximated to its final form while section 2 reached its maximum size as it contained all the exercises that appear in WSE as well as a number of others that were later discarded. Discussions of the differences between a *tool* and an *instrument* and between *consists of* and *is composed of* continued; the Expanded Definition section was completed and was only modified slightly in the light of that year's teaching experience; Nominal definitions were finally switched to the language laboratory; and Specific Definitions appeared in some numbers but were scattered through the Open exercises on General Definitions.

When I came to prepare a manuscript for the publishers I cut back the Classification exercises to the remaining exercise (ex 1) partly because I intended to have a section on Classification elsewhere – which regrettably never came about – and partly because I wanted to get on to definitions themselves as soon as possible. What remains at the end of the Introduction has all the signs of a feeble and unsatisfactory compromise. The slot-filling exercises 3 and 9, were finally abandoned in favour of the more timid choice requirement, but exercise 9 still remains rather a mess – no doubt, for one thing, whether all the sentences are definitions. The General and Expanded formulae were somewhat simplified – if that can be believed! – and most of the Open exercises (5, 7, 10, 14 and 17) were expanded to permit students to attempt only a proportion of the definitions in them. A display of the different grammatical features of definitions in English and Arabic was removed. The Specific Definitions were separated from the General Definitions (except number 10 in exercise 6, which unfortunately got left behind) and the formula for Specific Definitions appeared for the first time. Apart from this, the only new and untested part of the Unit was exercise 13, which was put in to make a more gradual transition between the display and the rather testing exercise 14.

REFERENCES

1 Swales, J., 'Introducing teachers to English for Science and Technology', *ELT Documents, 73/6.*

2 Barber, C. L., 'Some measurable characteristics of modern scientific prose' in *Contributions to English Syntax and Philology*, 1962.

3 Herbert, A. J., *The Structure of Technical English*, 1965.

4 Swales, J., 'Language Laboratory Materials and Service Courses: Problems of Tape Course Design for Science Students', *AVLJ*, VIII, I.

5 Owen, G. T., 'A Reading/Comprehension Course for Students of Science and Technology,' *ELT Documents*, 73/4.

6 Boyd, J. C. & Thorne, J. P., 'The Semantics of Modal Verbs', *Journal of Linguistics*, 5.

7 Lees, Robert B., *The Grammar of English Nominalisations*, 1963.

4

Teaching the Communicative Use of English

J. P. B. ALLEN AND H. G. WIDDOWSON

1 Introduction

In recent years, English language teaching overseas has taken on a new character. Previously it was usual to talk about the aims of English learning in terms of the so-called 'language skills' of speaking, understanding speech, reading and writing, and these aims were seen as relating to general education at the primary and secondary levels. Recently, however, a need has arisen to specify the aims of English learning more precisely as the language has increasingly been required to take on an auxiliary role at the tertiary level of education. English teaching has been called upon to provide students with the basic ability to use the language to receive, and (to a lesser degree) to convey information associated with their specialist studies. This is particularly so in the developing countries where essential textbook material is not available in the vernacular languages. Thus whereas one talked previously in general terms of ELT, we now have such acronymic variants as ESP (English for Special Purposes) and EST (English for Science and Technology).

This association of English teaching with specialist areas of higher education has brought into prominence a serious neglect of the needs of intermediate and advanced learners. Most of the improvements in language teaching methodology brought about during the last two decades have concentrated on the elementary syllabus. The reason for this is fairly clear: in any attempt to improve language teaching materials the logical place to start is at the beginning. Moreover, this approach ensures that the problems of organising language data are reduced to a minimum, since the course writer has a comparatively small number of words and structures to deal with in the early stages. The large amount of time and money that has been spent in developing elementary language teaching materials has produced impressive results, and a wide range of courses is now available to cater for the needs of students who are still in the process of acquiring a stock of basic vocabulary and simple grammatical structures. The teaching method which has proved most effective for this purpose contains two main ingredients: a step-by-step technique of structural grading, and a battery of intensive oral drills. Both features are based on the behaviourist doctrine that language learning consists primarily in establishing a set of habits, that is, a set of responses conditioned to occur with certain stimuli which may be either situations or words in a syntactic frame. Unfortunately, however, the generous provision of basic courses has coincided with a striking lack of new material specially designed for intermediate and advanced students. As a result, students who have become accustomed to an orderly progression of graded materials, simple explanations and easily-manipulated drills during the first two or three years of language learning find that these aids are suddenly withdrawn when they reach the end of the basic course, and that they are left to fend for themselves with little or no guidance at a time when the language is rapidly becoming more difficult. On the one hand we have an abundant supply of basic language courses, and on the other hand we have advanced teaching techniques (essay writing, report making, comprehension of complex reading material, etc.) designed for students who have a near-native competence in handling the target language, but there are virtually no materials to help the learner effect an orderly transition between these two extremes.

The general English instruction which is provided in secondary schools has in most cases proved to be inadequate as a preparation for the use which students are required to make of the language when they enter higher education. In consequence, many technical institutions and universities in developing countries provide courses with titles like 'Functional English', 'Technical English' and 'Report Writing', the purpose of which is to repair the deficiencies of secondary school teaching. However, such courses seldom recognise that a different approach may be needed to match the essentially different role which English assumes in higher education. They continue to treat English as a subject in its own right. It is true that there is some recognition of the auxiliary role it now has to play in that the selection of grammatical structures and lexical items to be taught are those which are of most frequent occurrence in the specialist literature with which the students are concerned. But the emphasis is still squarely on separate grammatical structures and lexical items, and such courses do little more than provide exercises in the manipulation of linguistic forms. The approach to English teaching is basically the same as that of the schools, and the assumption seems to be that it is likely to be more effective only because it is practised more efficiently. In fact, there is little evidence that such remedial courses are any more effective than the courses which they are intended to rectify.

The purpose of this paper is to suggest that what is needed is a different orientation to English study and to outline an approach which departs from that which is generally taken. Broadly, what is involved is a shift of the focus of attention from the grammatical to the communicative properties of the language. We take the view that the difficulties which the students encounter arise not so much from a defective knowledge of the system of English, but from an unfamiliarity with English use, and that consequently their needs cannot be met by a course which simply provides further practice in the composition of sentences, but only by one which develops a knowledge of how sentences are used in the performance of different communicative acts. The approach which we wish to outline here, then, represents an attempt to move from an almost exclusive concern with grammatical forms to at least an equal concern with rhetorical functions.

One might usefully distinguish two kinds of ability which an English course at this level should aim at developing. The first is the ability to recognise how sentences are used in the performance of acts of communication, the ability to understand the rhetorical functioning of language in use. The second is the ability to recognise and manipulate the formal devices which are used to combine sentences to create continuous passages of prose. We might say that the first has to do with the rhetorical coherence of *discourse*, and the second with the grammatical cohesion of *text*. In practice, of course, one kind of ability merges with the other, but in the form and function approach we are presenting here we focus on each of them in turn, while at the same time allowing for peripheral overlap.

2 The Use of Language in Discourse

Language considered as communication no longer appears as a separate subject but as an aspect of other subjects. A corollary to this is that an essential part of any subject is the manner in which its 'content' is given linguistic expression. Learning science, for example, is seen to be not merely a matter of learning facts, but of learning how language is used to give expression to certain reasoning processes, how it is used to define, classify, generalise, to make hypotheses, draw conclusions and so on. People who talk about 'scientific English' usually give the impression that it can be characterised in formal terms as revealing a high frequency of linguistic forms like the passive and the universal tense in association with a specialist vocabulary. But to characterise it in this way is to treat scientific discourse merely as exemplification of the language system, and does little or nothing to indicate what kind of communication it is.

The first principle of the approach we propose, then, is that the language should be presented in such a way as to reveal its character as communication. Let us consider how this principle might be put into practice. We will suppose that we are to design an English course for students of science in the first year of higher education.* We make two basic assumptions. Firstly, we assume that in spite of the shortcomings of secondary school English teaching the students have acquired considerable dormant competence in the manipulation of the language system. Secondly, we assume that they already have a knowledge of basic science. Hitherto, these two kinds of knowledge have existed in separation: our task is to relate them. We do this by composing passages on common topics in basic science and presenting them in such a way as to develop in the student an awareness of the ways in which the language system is used to express scientific facts and concepts. The passages are composed rather than derived directly from existing textbooks for two reasons. Firstly, we are able to avoid syntactic complexity and idiosyncratic features of style which would be likely to confuse students fresh from their experience of controlled and largely sentence-bound English instruction in schools, and/or deflect their attention from those features of use which we wish them to concentrate on. Our intention is to make linguistic forms as unobtrusive as possible. At the same time we wish to make their communicative function as obvious as possible, and this is the second reason for composing passages: we are able to 'foreground' features of language which have particular communicative value. It might be objected that the passages are not

---

* The examples of teaching material which appear in this paper are from a draft version of *English in Physical Science*. The *English in Focus* Series is published by OUP.

therefore representative of scientific writing. The answer to this is that they are representative of what we conceive to be certain basic communicative processes which underlie, and are variously realised in, individual pieces of scientific writing, and that they have been designed expressly to bring such processes more clearly into focus.

Each passage is provided with comprehension questions, but since we want to bring the student's attention to bear on his own reading activity as a process which involves a recognition of how language functions to convey information, the questions are not given at the end of the passage, as is the common practice, but are inserted into the passage itself. Furthermore, to ensure that the student is made aware of how the functioning of the language and his own understanding are related, solutions are provided for each comprehension question. These solutions are explanations in the sense that they make overt the kind of reasoning which underlies the ability to give the correct answer to the comprehension questions with which they are associated. Reasoning procedures such as are represented in these solutions might be said to be an essential element in any area of scientific enquiry, and their use here is intended to show the relevance of language to the study of science and to make appeal to the particular cognitive bent of science students.

The following is a sample of a passage composed and presented as described above. The sentences are numbered for ease of reference in the solutions, and in the exercises, which we shall discuss directly.

Matter and Volume

[1]Matter is the name given to everything which has weight and occupies space. [2]It may usually be detected by the senses of touch, sight or smell.

[3]Matter may exist in three states: solid, liquid and gas. [4]All substances, except those which decompose when heated, like wood, may be changed from one state into another. [5]A substance in the solid state may be changed into a liquid substance, and one in the liquid state may be changed into a gaseous substance. [6]Conversely, changes can take place in the reverse order: gases may be changed into liquids and liquids into solids. [7]A solid substance such as ice may be changed into the liquid state, or liquefied, to become water; and this may be changed into the gaseous state, or evaporated, to become steam. [8]Steam may also be converted into water and water into ice.

a)	Matter can usually be seen, smelt or touched.
b)	Matter can be seen, smelt and touched.
c)	All substances can be changed from one state into another.
d)	A liquid can be changed either into a gas or into a solid.

SOLUTIONS

a)   may = can
        may usually be detected by the senses of touch, sight or smell.
        (2)
    =   can usually be touched, seen or smelt.

    ∴ | Matter can usually be seen, smelt or touched. |

b)   touched, seen or smelt.
    =   *either* touched *or* seen *or* smelt.
  i.e. Some matter can be seen but not touched (e.g. visible gases)
        Some matter can be smelt but not seen (e.g. some invisible
        gases), etc.
        Matter can be seen, smelt and touched.
    =   *All* matter can be seen *and* smelt *and* touched.
    ∴   *It is NOT TRUE that matter can be seen, smelt and touched.*
c)   All substances, *except those which decompose when heated*,
        may be changed from one state to another. (4)
    ∴   Some substances cannot (= may not) change from one state
        to another.
    ∴   *It is NOT TRUE that all substances can be changed from one
        state to another.*
d)   A substance in the liquid state may be changed into a gaseous
        substance. (5)
  i.e. A liquid can be changed into a gas.
        gases may be changed into liquids and liquids [may be
        changed] into solids. (6)

    ∴ | A liquid can be changed *either* into a gas or into a solid. |

The purpose of the comprehension 'check' questions and the solutions is to draw the reader's attention to the process by which a piece of language is interpreted as discourse. The notes are meant to relate surface language forms to logical operations, and so to point to their communicative function in the passage concerned. It is likely that the student will know the meanings of such forms as elements of the language code: this kind of meaning, which we will call *signification*, can be exemplified by isolated sentences and is usually learned by pattern practice. What the student is less likely to recognise is the *value* which such items take on in utterances occurring within a context of discourse. For example, in the case of the passage just quoted, the student may know the signification of items like the articles, the quantifier *all* and the adverb *usually*. What the comprehension questions and solutions are intended to draw out is the value such terms have in the making of statements of different kinds: generalisations, qualifications and so on, which set up implicational relations with other parts of the discourse. When a qualification is signalled by the use of *usually*, for example, we need to recognise not only that the sentence in itself has a particular rhetorical value, but also that it has a rhetorical relation with preceding and succeeding sentences.

This focus on communicative value is also a feature of the exercises which follow the notes. The first of these draws the student's attention to anaphoric devices. Such devices, of course, are capable of a very wide range of values. The so-called 'demonstrative pronouns' *this* and *these*, for example, are generally given an 'ostensive' signification which associates them with singular and plural noun phrases: in the early lessons of an English course they occur in sentences such as 'This is a book' 'These are books' and as pro-forms they usually make no further appearance in the course. In actual discourse, however, it is not always easy to recognise which noun phrase, or phrases, such pro-forms are to be related to since they do not appear in neat equative sentences such as are presented in the early English lessons. The reader has to select the appropriate value from a number of alternatives, all of which are grammatically possible. Furthermore, it commonly happens that *this* does not relate to a noun phrase at all, but to some superordinate notion which is not given overt expression as such in the discourse. Thus, it may take on the value 'the fact X', 'the set of facts X, Y, Z', 'the idea X', 'the set of ideas X, Y, Z', 'the argument X', 'the set of arguments X, Y, Z' and so on, where X, Y, Z are elements in the preceding discourse. To recognise the value of *this* in such cases the reader has to understand the communicative intention expressed through the choice of particular surface forms.

The passage cited above would be an early one in the course we have in mind and so contains no instance of the use of *this* to refer to a superordinate notion. It is better to lead up to the 'superordinate' use of *this* by getting the student to recognise first the simpler operations of anaphora. One way of doing this (where *this* = 'the ability to recognise the simpler operations of anaphora'!) is by drawing the student's attention directly to features of anaphora in the passage by means of an exercise of the following kind:

EXERCISE A: PRONOUN REFERENCE

1 In sentence 2, *It* refers to:
  a) Weight
  b) Space
  c) Matter
2 In sentence 5, *one* refers to:
  a) A substance
  b) A substance in the solid state
  c) A liquid substance
3 In sentence 7, *this* refers to:
  a) A solid substance
  b) Water
  c) Ice

Another difficulty which learners have in understanding discourse is in recognising when different expressions have equivalent contextual value. Learners may have their attention drawn to the way different forms function as expressions in a particular passage by means of an exercise of the following kind:

EXERCISE B: REPHRASING

Replace the expressions in italics in the following sentences with expressions from the text which have the same meaning.

1 *A substance in the solid state* may be changed into *a liquid substance*.
2 *Gases* may be changed into *liquids* and *liquids* may be changed into *solids*.
3 A solid may be *changed into the liquid state*.
4 A liquid may be *changed* into a gas.

So far we have been principally concerned with getting the learner to recognise the communicative value of expressions which correspond with sentence constituents. We may now introduce exercises which focus on the way sentences themselves function as communicative acts within the discourse. Our interest now is in the illocutionary force of the sentences which are used. (Austin, 1962, Searle, 1969). We want to get the learner to see that understanding a passage of English involves the recognition of what illocutionary acts are performed in it. One way of doing this is to ask him to insert expressions into the sentences of the passage which make explicit what their illocutionary function is. Thus in a sentence which is being used as an illustrative statement, *for example* can be inserted; in one which serves as a classification, one can insert the performative verb *classify*, and so on. An exercise of this kind based on the passage given might be as follows:

EXERCISE C: RELATIONSHIPS BETWEEN STATEMENTS

Place the following expressions in the sentences indicated. Replace and re-order the words in the sentence where necessary:

a) can be defined as (1)
b) for example (4)
c) thus (5)
d) also (6)
e) thus (6)
f) for example (7)
g) then (7)
h) conversely (8)

The three types of exercise which have been proposed are graded in the sense that they are designed to make increasing demands on the learner's own writing ability. Exercise A, like the comprehension check questions, involves no writing at all. Exercise B is a simple copying exercise, the purpose of which is to reinforce the reader's perception of certain discourse functions. Exercise C requires the reader to use his knowledge of the language productively: he has to insert the given expressions in the correct places and to make structural alterations where necessary in the sentences concerned. This grading is intended to effect a gradual transfer from receptive awareness to productive ability.

We may now continue to provide writing practice based on the reading passage. But we wish to do this not as a meaningless manipulation of sentence patterns, but as a use of English in the performance of different communicative acts relevant to the learner's special subject of study. We want to preserve the rhetorical orientation we have adopted, and keep the learner's attention focussed on language in use. In Exercise C our purpose was to get the learner to make acts like defining and illustrating explicit. Now we want to get him to perform such acts himself. This might be brought about by an exercise of the following kind, which combines control with the sort of scope for mental activity which might be expected to appeal to the kind of learner we are concerned with, and which brings the language being learnt into close association with the subject for which it serves as medium. The exercise is based on the continuation of the reading passage quoted above, which provides the information necessary to complete the diagram.

EXERCISE D: STATEMENTS BASED ON DIAGRAMS

1 Write out a complete version of the following diagram by filling in the spaces.

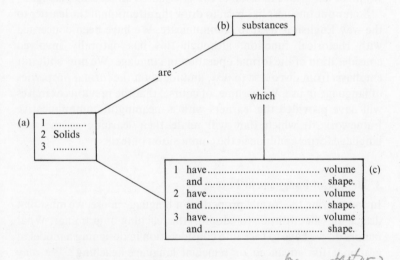

2 Use the completed diagram to:
  (i) Write definitions, by using boxes (a), (b) and (c)
      EXAMPLE:
      Solids are substances which have a definite volume and a definite shape.
  (ii) Write *generalisations*, by using boxes (a) and (c)
      EXAMPLE:
      Solids have a definite volume and a definite shape.

Exercise D reflects the importance we attach to the presentation of language as an essential aspect of the scientific subject which the learner is studying. The purpose of the approach we are illustrating here is to get the learner to recognise how the language and 'subject matter', commonly considered in isolation, are interrelated in acts of communication. We may promote this purpose further by following up Exercise D with exercises which present a problem requiring reference to knowledge of both language and of 'subject matter' for its solution. One might, for example, get the learner to produce definitions and generalisations relating to another content area by asking him first to reduce the essential information to tabular form. Again, one could get him to draw a simple diagram of a machine, or a flow-chart of a process as a preliminary to providing a verbal description. Given any scientific or technical field, it is not difficult to think of relevant problems which would serve to integrate the student's knowledge of language and 'subject matter', and which would be a logical extension of exercises based on reading passages.

So far our business has been to draw the attention of the learner to the way English is used to communicate. We have been concerned with rhetorical function, although this has naturally involved consideration of the formal operation of language. We now shift our emphasis from discourse to text, and focus on the formal properties of language in use. We assume, of course, that the previous exercises will have provided the learners with a meaningful communicative framework to which they will relate their learning of the way language forms combine in the composition of texts.

3 The Use of Language in Text

In considering the formal properties of language in use, we must first decide on what attitude to adopt to the teaching of grammar. What factors do we have to take into consideration in designing a model of grammar for advanced or remedial language teaching? We may assume, firstly, that a pedagogic grammar for advanced learners must provide the student with fresh and stimulating material. As was suggested earlier in this paper, there is no point in presenting a remedial English class at the University level with a speeded-up version of the secondary school syllabus, for the class will rapidly become bored and resentful even if they show evidence of not having fully mastered the material. The rejection by students of the rapid repeat technique of remedial teaching is a familiar experience in higher education, and should occasion no surprise. Not only do advanced learners have a natural reluctance to cover familiar ground for the second or third time, they have, in fact, reached a stage in their studies when they may no longer be able to benefit from the oral, inductive type of teaching employed at a more elementary level. As was pointed out earlier, it is this fact that prompts us to propose an approach which gives recognition to the real needs of advanced students. It must be stressed that the task for the advanced learner is not simply to experience more language material, but to develop a complex set of organisational skills over and above those which he needed to cope with the elementary syllabus, and to learn to put these to use in serving a variety of communicative purposes. One difference between elementary and advanced courses lies in the fact that students at an advanced level have had a good deal of instruction in grammar and, as was suggested earlier, are likely to possess considerable dormant competence in English. It follows that one of the principal aims of advanced language teaching should be to activate this competence, and to extend it, by leading the student to relate his previously-acquired linguistic knowledge to meaningful realisations of the language system in passages of immediate relevance to his professional interests or specialised field of studies.

A second consideration is that the information in a pedagogic grammar must be relevant to a learner's needs. In order to ensure this we must insist on a clear distinction between linguistic and pedagogic grammars. A linguistic grammar is concerned with a specification of the formal properties of a language, while the purpose of a pedagogic grammar is to help a learner acquire a practical mastery of a language. There is no reason for supposing that the two types of statement will bear any overt resemblance to one another. It is particularly important that this principle should be clearly stated at a time when many teachers and textbook writers are turning to linguistics as a source of ideas about how to handle language in the classroom. In general, we expect that a knowledge of linguistic grammars will provide teachers with pedagogically useful insights into language structure, but we do not expect that the content of a linguistic grammar will be reflected in any direct or systematic way in a pedagogic grammar based on it. A further principle is that pedagogic grammars are typically eclectic. By this we mean that the applied linguist must pick and choose among formal statements in the light of his experience as a teacher, and decide what are pedagogically the most appropriate ways of arranging the information that he derives from linguistic grammars. Thus, we expect that the insights incorporated in a pedagogic grammar will be drawn from a number of linguistic models, and that the teaching materials will be judged solely in terms of whether or not they promote quick and efficient learning in the student.

As already stated, we assume that the students have some knowledge of how the language works, which derives from pedagogic grammar. We also assume that this knowledge will be consolidated as the students experience language used in meaningful contexts. For these reasons we have not attempted to provide a detailed review of English grammar. Instead, the grammar exercises are designed to focus on points which are particularly important in scientific writing, especially those which may represent continuing 'trouble spots' for many students. Wherever possible we aim to avoid the more mechanical types of substitution drill. The whole approach we adopt in this paper is based on the assumption that the students will be people whose minds are directed towards rational thought and problem-solving, and the grammar exercises are designed to take this fact into account. Wherever possible, we have here, as elsewhere, used exercises which we hope will require the same kind of thinking that science students would naturally be engaged in as part of their specialist studies. The following examples show how we have attempted to provide grammar practice in a meaningful way, and without losing sight of the natural communicative use of language.

EXERCISE E: DEFINITIONS IN SCIENTIFIC DISCOURSE

Definitions in scientific discourse often take the following forms:

(a) $\text{A} \begin{Bmatrix} \text{is/are} \\ \text{may be defined as} \end{Bmatrix} \text{B which C}$

E.g.   A thermometer *is* an instrument *which* is used for measuring temperatures.

A thermometer *may be defined as* an instrument *which* is used for measuring temperatures.

(b) $\text{B which C} \begin{Bmatrix} \text{is/are called} \\ \text{is/are known as} \end{Bmatrix} \text{A}$

E.g.   An instrument *which* is used for measuring temperatures *is called* a thermometer.

An instrument *which* is used for measuring temperatures *is known as* a thermometer.

Expand the following into full definitions. Write each sentence twice, using any of the patterns illustrated above.

1 Metamorphosis/the physical transformation/is undergone by various animals during development after the embryonic state.
2 Metals/the class of chemical elements/are characterised by ductility, malleability, lustre and conductivity.

EXERCISE F: FORMATION OF THE IMPERSONAL PASSIVE

Write down the passive version of all the active sentences. Then combine the passive sentences, following the clues provided in the box.

Active: we may show the expansion of a gas
Passive: the expansion of a gas _ _ _ _ _ _ _ _ _ _ _ _ _ _ _
Active: we heat the gas
Passive: the gas _ _ _ _ _ _ _ _ _ _
Active: we demonstrate an apparatus in Figure 41
Passive: an apparatus _ _ _ _ _ _ _ _ _ _ _ in Figure 41

The expansion of a gas when it _ _ _ _ _ _ _ _ _ _ _ _ may
_ _ _ _ _ _ _ _ _ _ _ _ _ by the apparatus _ _ _ _ _ _
in Figure 41

EXERCISE G: TIME EXPRESSIONS

(i) Rewrite the sentences, selecting one of the time expressions and putting it at the beginning of the sentence. The time expression you select should be the one which corresponds most closely to the meaning of the words in italics, which should be omitted.
  1 The water vapour condenses to water *as a result* it is able to fall downwards as rain or snow (when, before).
  2 The aluminium is in the measuring cylinder *during this time* we may measure the volume of water displaced (as soon as, while)
  3 *First* the water is forced out of the ballast tanks by compressed air *before this* the submarine is not able to rise to the surface (until, when)
(ii) Compare the following sentences with your answer in Part (i). If the sentences have approximately the same meaning, put a tick in the box; if not, put a cross.
  1 Water vapour can fall as rain or snow but the vapour must condense to water first. ☐
  2 A volume of water is displaced and as a result we can put the aluminium in the measuring cylinder. ☐
  3 A submarine is not able to rise to the surface while the ballast tanks are full of water. ☐

It may seem to some that exercises based on a surface structure approach constitute a return to outmoded principles. There is an important issue at stake here, which we touched on earlier in our discussion of the distinction between linguistics and pedagogic grammars. A number of recent publications have shown a tendency to assume that the latest developments in linguistic theory should at all costs be reflected in language teaching materials. But it is not always the latest linguistic model which provides the most satisfactory basis for the preparation of teaching materials. For example, the relevant treatment of transformations for our purpose appears to be that of Zellig Harris rather than Chomsky. For Harris, transformational analysis is a logical extension of constituent analysis, and is based on the same criteria of form and distribution. Transformations are set up formally as a relation between text-sentences, and not in the form of instructions for generating sentences, as in Chomsky's theory. A pedagogically useful consequence is that we can distinguish well-established transformations from those which are barely acceptable or used only in particular linguistic environments. Moreover, Harris's transformational rules are relevant to the notion of communicative competence, and therefore seem to be a more suitable basis for teaching material than Chomsky's transformations, which operate without reference to context.

4 Methods of Teaching the Writing Skill

In the classroom it is not always easy to devise situations which call for genuine written communication, so that students can express themselves in a natural way in response to a real need. One method of making writing meaningful is to get the learner to 'talk to himself' on paper. This approach, generally known as 'creative writing' has been widely advocated in L_1 teaching situations as a substitute for formal essays which fail because the task is boring and artificial. Creative writing clearly has a general educational value, but its usefulness is limited in that it tends to produce an intensely personal style, in fact a type of literature, which has little or no social function. Advocates of this approach believe that the skill developed in creative writing carries over into institutional writing without the need for further instruction, but this claim is not substantiated by the evidence so far available. On the face of it, it seems unlikely that a student who has been encouraged to express himself through the medium of prose poems will be able to turn his hand readily to the production of business correspondence or an academic treatise, without some explicit instruction in the conventions which govern these particular styles of writing. A second limitation is that the creative writing approach is restricted to an L_1 learning situation. If an L_2 student wishes to express himself 'creatively' he will normally turn to his mother tongue. He needs the target language in order to read textbooks, write summaries and reports, and participate in routine professional or social conversations, all of which are examples of the institutional use of language, which require a mastery of the appropriate conventions.

A variation of the creative writing approach is found in many American textbooks designed for use with freshman composition classes. These books devote much space to the discussion of such traditional principles of rhetoric as coherence, unity and emphasis, the classical structure of the oration and an analysis of the various types of discourse (exposition, argument, description, narration, etc.). The authors of some composition handbooks include the rudiments of formal logic, in the belief that patterns of proof can be used as an aid in the organisation of paragraphs and in checking for weak points in an argument once it has been written. Such books are based on the assumption that it helps a learner if he understands the potentialities of written language and is familiar with some of the rhetorical devices that fluent writers habitually use. However, it is doubtful whether an *analysis* of other people's writing can in itself produce fluent writers. What the learner needs, especially in an L_2 situation, is a form of exercise which will help him to achieve a *synthesis* of many disparate grammatical and lexical elements in the form of a coherent composition of his own. One problem in achieving this type of synthesis in the classroom is to find the right combination of freedom and control: enough control to ensure that the student's composition does not degenerate into a mass of mistakes, and enough freedom for the student to exercise his own judgement and thereby to learn something instead of merely copying. Various attempts have been made to provide guided practice developing into free composition. The materials available fall into four main categories, and we will examine a representative example from each category.

SUBSTITUTION IN FRAMES

Example: K. W. Moody (1966). Moody's frames are akin to the familiar substitution table in which interchangeable elements are grouped in columns, but whereas most substitution tables represent the structure of a single sentence, in this case the frames are arranged in a series, so that a succession of choice from left to right will result in a paragraph, letter or short composition. The selection of alternatives is not entirely automatic; the structural patterns are fixed but the choice of lexical items is determined by the student. When he begins this series of exercises the student does not have to worry about the choice of grammatical patterns or the way in which sentences interrelate, but he has to think about the meaning of what he is writing and he must ensure that his lexical choices produce a composition that makes sense. The exercises are arranged in four stages to give the student progressively more freedom of choice. At the first stage the sets of alternatives in the frames are written out in full, and the student's problem is mainly one of lexical collocation. Each exercise at Stage 1 is matched with a Stage 2 exercise in which the frame is repeated but with a number of blanks. The purpose of this is to give the learner some opportunity of using his own choice of words, once he has achieved control over the structural patterns of the paragraph. At Stage 3 the student has even more freedom of choice, since only a few words are retained from the original frame. At Stage 4 he is asked to write a paragraph of his own, along the lines suggested by the earlier exercises, but without the frame to guide him. At the final stage, therefore, the student has a free choice of words and structures, but he has been led into free composition gradually and he should retain a clear idea of the paragraph outline from earlier stages of the practice.

SAMPLE COMPOSITION WITH SELECTIVE STRUCTURE PRACTICE

Example: T. C. Jupp and John Milne (1968). As in the case of Moody, the aim is to provide students who are learning composition writing with detailed guidance in language and subject matter, but at the same time to leave them with the opportunity for personal expression. With this second approach, however, the element of control is more relaxed and the student is encouraged to make his own selection of words and structures throughout the practice. The Jupp and Milne sequence is arranged in four stages. Stage 1 consists of a statement of the subject of the composition, e.g.: 'Write about a very important examination, interview or meeting which you once went to. Carefully describe your feelings and thoughts, and say what happened.' Stage 2 consists of oral and written structure practice, the aim of which is to make students proficient in the use of those structures which he is likely to need in order to write about the set topic. A few new patterns are introduced in each unit, but most of the structure practice consists of a revision of patterns which have been previously learned. It is a feature of this material that the structures practised are grouped according to topic rather than being determined by an abstract linguistic scheme of grading. At Stage 3, having been well primed by class discussion and by structure drills, the student reads a sample composition in which the set topic is handled in a context familiar to the authors (in this case, an account of an entrance examination at Cambridge). The structures that the students have been practising are exemplified in the sample composition. Finally, at Stage 4, the student is instructed to (a) write down some sentences from the structure practice; (b) carefully re-read the sample composition, noting examples of relevant structures; (c) write a composition of his own, referring if necessary to the sample composition and making sure that he uses examples of the practised structures; (d) give the finished composition to a friend to read.

MODIFICATION OF MODEL PARAGRAPHS

Example: Dykstra, Port and Port (1966). These materials consist of a collection of 42 passages all concerned with the adventures of Ananse the spider, a character in West African folklore. Using these passages as a basis, the student is required to perform a series of operations, including structural modification and lexical insertion, in a series of graduated steps, beginning with relatively mechanical operations and proceeding as quickly as possible to the most advanced steps, which represent free creative composition. The materials are arranged in such a way that they represent a roughly programmed course which can be useful to students who have attained different levels of control over writing in English. The following instructions, all quoted from the text, show the types of activity involved. The numbers indicate grading in difficulty on a scale 1–58. The operations listed can be performed on any of 42 passages, and usually more than one operation is performed on a single passage.

  1 Copy the passage.
  4 Rewrite the entire passage changing *Ananse* to *the spiders*. Change the pronouns where necessary.
 14 Rewrite the entire passage in the active voice.
 36 Rewrite the entire passage adding adjective clauses beginning with *who*, *which* or *that* after the following words: *young man*, *mother*, *village*, etc.

58 Create a folktale of your own about Ananse the spider. Use between 100 and 150 words in your tale.

The three types of guided composition exercise summarised above are all based on the notion of parallel texts. This approach is successful so long as the student's writing is restricted to short letters, folktales, personal histories or other stereotyped formulas. However, the parallel text approach tends to break down if the student has to handle scientific subjects, since in this type of writing the arguments are highly specific and each text must be regarded as unique. The guided composition method discussed below involves the intensive study of a single text, and is suitable for use in the context of scientific writing where parallel texts are difficult to devise.

GUIDED PARAGRAPH BUILDING

The exercise is done in four stages. At the first stage the student examines various groups of words and combines each group into a sentence by following the clues provided. Some sentences are easy to write, some are more difficult; this reflects the situation in actual writing, where simple sentences alternate with more complex structures according to the nature of the message the writer wishes to convey. At the second stage the student creates a coherent paragraph by rewriting the sentences in a logical order, adding various 'transitional' features where necessary. Thirdly, the student checks his work against a version of the paragraph incorporated into a free reading passage elsewhere in the book. The paragraph writing is designed to allow some scope for the student to exercise his own judgement, so there is no reason why the student's version should be identical to the one in the book. If the paragraphs differ, the student should try to evaluate the relative merits of the two versions. At the fourth stage the student writes the paragraph again in a free style of his own devising, based on a set of notes which are similar to the rough jottings made by an author when he is sketching out a plan for a paragraph. Thus the student is led by stages to the point where he should be able to write a paragraph of his own, in a way which seeks to imitate some of the processes of real-life composition.

The following paragraph writing exercise illustrates this procedure.

A Join each of the groups of words below into one sentence, using the additional material in the box. Words in italics should be omitted. Number your sentences and begin each one with a capital letter.

1 an acid will *affect* litmus
   an acid will react with washing soda
   it will give off carbon dioxide

   > turn/red/and/it/,/giving

2 the metal disappears
   hydrogen is liberated

   > and

3 one class of bases *is* called alkalis
   they will dissolve in water
   they will form solutions
   they will *affect* red litmus

   > special/,/,/and/which/turn/blue

4 an acid is a compound
   it will attack some metals
   it will liberate hydrogen
   magnesium is dissolved in it

   > containing hydrogen/which/and/when

5 alkalis forms solutions
   they feel soapy
   they will dissolve substances
   they are used in various cleaning processes

   > which/and which/oily and greasy/,/and for this reason/
   > frequently

6 acids *burn* substances
   wood paper cloth human skin

   > have a burning effect on/like/,/,/and

B Create a coherent paragraph by rewriting the eleven sentences in a logical order.* Before you write the paragraph, add the following material to the sentences.

> 2 in the latter case
> 6 a further characteristic of acids is that they

C When you have written your paragraph, re-read it and make sure that the sentences are presented in a logical order. Give the paragraph a suitable title. Check with the version given in the back of the book and correct if necessary. (It is possible to write this paragraph in more than one way.)

D Read through the paragraph again. Make sure you know all the words, using a dictionary if necessary. Without referring to your previous work rewrite the paragraph using the following clues:

compounds – divided – acids – bases – salts
acid – compound of hydrogen – attack metals – liberate hydrogen – magnesium dissolved
acid – litmus red – washing soda – carbon dioxide
burn substances – wood, paper, etc.
base – oxides, hydroxides – neutralise acids – salt-like substances
alkalis – solutions – soapy – dissolve oil – grease – cleaning
salt – product, acid neutralised – metal dissolved
metal disappears – hydrogen liberated
salt – substance – metal takes place of hydrogen

5 Conclusion

In this paper we have suggested an approach to the teaching of English which recognises that the acquisition of receptive and productive knowledge of a language must involve the learning of rules of use as well as rules of grammar. Many students who enter higher education have had experience only of the latter and are consequently unable to deal with English when it is used in the normal process of communication. What we have attempted to do is to show how rules of use might be taught, both those which have to do with the communicative properties of discourse and those which

---

* Five groups of words have been omitted.

have to do with the formal properties of texts. We make no claim that the kind of exercises which we have illustrated here are in any sense definitive: other, and no doubt more effective, exercises might be devised. We believe, however, that such exercises should take into account the needs of the students and the nature of the abilities which must be developed to meet them, and be related therefore to the kind of theoretical considerations within the context of which we have placed the exercises presented here. There are signs that linguists are now turning their attention to the communicative properties of language and the functioning of language in social contexts. We have said that it is a mistake for the language teacher to assume that he must automatically adjust his pedagogy to conform to the latest linguistic fashion, but in this case it is necessary for the language teacher to emulate the linguist by considering communicative functions as well as, and in relation to, linguistic forms. Such a shift in focus is warranted not by the practice of the linguist but by the essential needs of the language learner.

REFERENCES

Austin, J. L., *How to Do Things with Words*, The Clarendon Press: Oxford, 1962.

Dykstra, G., Port, R. and Port, A., *A Course in Controlled Composition: Ananse Tales*, New York: Teachers College Press, 1966.

Jupp, T. C. and Milne, J., *Guided Course in English Composition*. London: Heinemann, 1968.

Moody, K. W., *Written English Under Control*. Ibadan: Oxford University Press, 1966.

Searle, J. R., *Speech Acts*. Cambridge: Cambridge University Press, 1969.

5

Writing 'Nucleus'

M. BATES

1 Outline

The ESP materials now being published under the title of *Nucleus* consist of an introductory 'core' course (*General Science*) and a number of specific courses for different branches of science and technology. Each course has the same structure of 12 units plus 3 short revision units, and follows the same notional syllabus aimed at introducing the student to the realisation of essential scientific concepts and their application to his own subject. Each unit of the *General Science* course presents and practises the concept within settings drawn from basic science or everyday life. The aim of these productive exercises, which rely a good deal on visual support, is to activate the student's knowledge of English and to encourage him to communicate about scientific and factual matters in interesting ways. This is a preparation for the parallel unit of his subject-specific course, which concentrates on reading and listening exercises. Each specific unit, however, begins with a series of productive exercises in which the concept presented in the general unit is applied to appropriate topics and contexts within the subject; these active exercises lead in to the study of written and aural texts.

2 Origins

The materials evolved out of a teaching situation which may have parallels with many others where students of science and technology are being introduced to the English of their subject under difficult circumstances; these difficult circumstances including a limited and inappropriate knowledge of English at entry, attitudes to language-learning which placed little emphasis on practical use, low motivation and a divorce between the language-teaching situation and the eventual uses of English, which were often difficult to specify exactly.

3 The Learning Situation

The University of Tabriz (now Azerabadegan), Iran, where the series was designed, had a large proportion of students of scientific and technological disciplines. These included the Faculties of Engineering (Civil, Mechanical, Electrical, Production, Agriculture, Medicine, Pharmacy and Science (Physics, Chemistry, Mathematics, Biology, Geology). Students began to specialise in their subject from the first year, unlike in certain other Third World universities, where students begin with a generalised study of science before splitting into Engineering, Physics etc. The linguistic situation was somewhat complex. The medium of instruction was Persian, the language of education at all levels and the only native language used in the written form, but not the mother-tongue of the 40 per cent or so of Azerbaijani students, who spoke a Turkic language. The fact that many students were bilingual (trilingual in the case of a few, e.g. Armenians and Assyrians) did not seem to affect their ability to learn English. Most of the science and technology lectures were thus given in Persian. There were a number of foreign lecturers – Indian, Pakistani, British and American – who attempted to use English as a medium, with little success except to the most advanced classes. Some Indian and Pakistani lecturers learnt enough Persian to get by; others had to resort to such compromises as addressing the class through an interpreter or handing out translations of their lectures.

For reading matter the students in the early stages of their four-year degree courses relied on cyclostyled sheets and booklets ('poly-copies'), containing potted information often translated from foreign textbooks. They began to use English language textbooks in their second or third year but, like the use of English-medium lectures, this was somewhat random and varied from subject to subject. In Pharmacy, for example, students used English textbooks even in their first year. Some of these books were prescribed, others were optional. Some students had difficulty in gaining access to foreign language books. Some might be using British or American textbooks, which might or might not be at the appropriate level of specialisation, and there was no guarantee that students in the same class were using the same books. The most popular books were the cheapest: Russian textbooks translated into English and published in the Soviet Union. This gives some indication of the problems involved in investigating the English language reading and aural learning needs of the students: not only were there the usual variations in language use depending on subject, level and medium; there was also considerable extra stylistic diversity including features of Indian spoken English and Russian written English. These problems were aggravated by the fact that our service English courses were given in the first and second years, whereas most students did not experience a really urgent need for English until the latter part of their course.

The method of study, especially in the initial stages, depended a good deal on memorisation of 'polycopies' under the pressure of examinations. When the film *Fahrenheit 451* was shown in Tabriz, the most memorable part for me was the final scene in which the exiles walk to and fro under the trees committing to memory the precious and vulnerable knowledge contained in the books which they have saved from destruction. This was very like the scene at the University in the weeks preceding an examination. The traditional method of learning no doubt affected the attitudes of students to English: they were predisposed to view it as a *content* subject rather than as a *means* of communicating and acquiring knowledge. The design of the Tabriz materials attempted to take account of both traditional attitudes to learning and the fact that students were attending English classes in order to acquire 'communication skills'. I should add that many students responded well to the more open-ended, problem-solving features of their language course, often showing a readiness to think for themselves and improvise; perhaps this was because the activities marked a welcome change from their previous experience of language-learning.

Because of the dependence on memorising texts about their subject, the study of science and technology tended to concentrate on theory in the initial stages. Even students of applied sciences had little experience, if any, of laboratory or workshop. This was a factor to take into account when using scientific equipment and other *realia* in the teaching of EST.

Another feature of academic life affected the students' attitudes to learning English – the interdisciplinary rivalry. Certain subjects (those leading to well-paid jobs) were considered intrinsically 'better' than others. On the whole, I think the effect of these attitudes on learning was harmful for all disciplines. Students who belonged to the prestigious faculties were conscious of their own importance and scornful of other subjects. Those studying other subjects often felt little enthusiasm for them and at the end of the first year re-sat the entrance examination in an attempt to qualify for a subject with more kudos (thus physicists tried to get into engineering, biologists into medicine). The effects on language-teaching were, firstly, that many students were hypersensitive about the relevance of the materials to their own subject (for example, engineers revolted if they thought they were having to read about physics) and, secondly, that those who failed to reach their cherished subject (as many did) became disillusioned and less responsive to learning in the second year. There was little opportunity for interdisciplinary study or collaboration; even some of the foreign language teachers became infected by these divisive rivalries.

4 The Teaching Situation

The science and technology sections of the University had expanded rapidly in the '50's and '60's. The Language Centre was set up in 1970 in order to cater for the special language needs of these students. The English Department continued to run remedial classes in the Faculty of Letters, but eventually the Language Centre served all other disciplines, including Nursing Science and Education. The Language Centre also expanded rapidly and by 1972–3, when the *Nucleus* approach was being thought out, it had a staff of over 20.

Most of the teachers of English attached to the Language Centre were British; a few were American. The fact that there was only one Iranian lecturer was a disadvantage for us; most Iranian English teachers held the belief, still prevalent in many parts of the world, that traditional English language and literature teaching was academically more respectable than English for Special Purposes; they preferred to remain in the Faculty of Letters, even though the actual standard of English at entry tended to be lower there.

The Language Centre taught six hours per week of English to the First Year and three hours to the Second Year. When the Centre was first set up, the methods and materials used varied greatly. Various published courses which were then available were tried out, but most of them were found unsuitable even on purely structural criteria, either because the texts were too long and complex or because the language and contexts were so simplified and non-specific as to be uncharacteristic of 'scientific English'. One of the more helpful books was *Writing Scientific English* by Swales, parts of which were used in the Second Year. Although our students did not need primarily to write English, many of the exercises seemed to concentrate on important aspects of scientific communication appropriate for receptive learning also. Many teachers, however, preferred to write their own texts, doctored and simplified to illustrate particular sentence-structures and vocabulary. Tony Dudley-Evans and Tim Smart produced whole courses for Engineering on these lines. The specialised language work was supplemented by unrelated 'general English', usually through *Practice and Progress* by L. G. Alexander. At the opposite extreme to this, one teacher attempted to read through a Pharmacology textbook (undoctored) with a Pharmacy class. But, despite the obvious relevance to the students' needs, the class got through only four pages before seizing up with a surfeit of vocabulary.

5   Basic Criteria for Course Development

During and partly as a result of these experiments with traditional materials, certain criteria for the development of a new approach began to crystallise, which were to form the basis of the *Nucleus* approach:

1   An integrated framework for the teaching of English to students of different subjects was felt to be necessary; this should both allow for adequate diversification between disciplines (with teachers and writers specialising in the subjects they were interested in) and enable teachers to pool their ideas, coordinate their efforts and economise on the limited time available for writing and research.

2   The material had to be attractive to the students both by being clearly related to their academic needs and by containing interesting learning activities.

3   Most of the students could not handle the continuous, complicated discourse of their textbooks. They became mesmerised by the technical vocabulary and balked by the involved syntax. They were also untrained in recognising the rhetorical organisation, information structure and logical interrelationships of a text. They did not seem to benefit much from repetitive drilling of verb-forms and sentence-structures. These activities were not particularly motivating, they ignored the grammatical and semantic patterning of continuous discourse and they took too long to get anywhere. An approach to text was needed which progressed rapidly from simple utterances to longer stretches of discourse. At the early stages there should be plenty of active use of English, encouraging students to participate, giving them confidence and a feel for the communicative value of the language, which would lead into 'passive' reading and listening

exercises. Hence the decision to precede texts with rapid productive exercises preparing the students to handle the key concepts contained in them.

4 Because of the aptitude of many students for memorisation and repetition, the material had to include some relatively 'mechanical' exercises as well as more open-ended communicative activities. Hence the combination of slot-filling and sentence-completion techniques with problem-solving, discussion etc.

6 The Students

A few more words about the students and language-teachers may be illuminating before I go on to describe the development of the materials in detail.

The standard of English at entry varied considerably but was generally low. The students' previous experience of English had placed much emphasis on grammatical rules and paradigms. Few students had had any opportunity to use the grammatical forms which they had learned in any communicative sense. For example, although many could recite the past forms of irregular verbs, few if any could produce them appropriately in continuous speech.

Despite their limited knowledge of English, most of the students were eager, at least in their first year, to improve and apply what they knew. Motivation was strong, at least in two, sometimes contrary, directions: towards making 'conversation' and towards reading about their subject. They were generally cheerful, humorous and extrovert, and responded readily to such novel language-learning procedures as miming the revolutions of electrons round an atom and being human chessmen moving on the tiled floor to demonstrate the meaning of prepositions of direction.

Relations between students and foreign language teachers were generally good. I believe that this contributed to the success of the materials and that, conversely, the interest and novelty of the materials helped to foster a teacher–student rapport. Classes were usually of between 20 and 30 students; we did not have the problem of mixed discipline groups.

7 The Teachers and Writers

Most of the teachers approached the task of writing our own ESP course with enthusiasm. Many of us were recently refreshed by courses in TEFL or Applied Linguistics. These had had a beneficial effect on our curiosity and application, although they also implanted some bad effects – confusion over terminology and assumptions of rival academic schools, which may have set up false dichotomies. A few of us had past experience of ESP but we were handicapped by lack of scientific training. Our academic backgrounds ranged from Psychology and Sociology through English and Modern Languages to Classics. The teacher who was closest to having a prior knowledge of his subject was Ian Stewart who wrote part of the Geology course and had a Geography degree. Thus, we were typical of ESP teachers in many parts of the world. On the other hand, teachers became rapidly interested in the subject which they specialised in. This was made possible by dividing up the writing tasks according to subject. Those who taught English for a particular discipline (usually a pair of teachers) would also write the materials for it. This ensured continuous feedback on the effectiveness of materials. (A book was kept in which teachers could register their impressions of teachability, effectiveness and student reaction immediately after giving the lesson.)

8 Constraints on the Definition of Goals

In developing the materials, some of us were hampered by lack of appropriate textbooks at the required level, which was taken in the first year to be somewhere between the 'Ordinary' and 'Advanced' levels of the British General Certificate of Education. Establishing the appropriate level for the content of the courses was not easy. We were limited in our own knowledge and access to books. A basic assumption was that most if not all of the topics and contexts used should be familiar to the students, which meant that in the early stages we had to restrict ourselves to what they had studied in the Secondary Schools. Ideally, it should have also meant that later stages would be linked to the subject-syllabus. In practice, however, the syllabus seemed to be somewhat fluid and unpredictable and we were hampered in gaining access to it by our lack of 'Persian for Academic Purposes', since most of the lecturers and administrators did not speak EAP. I gained most of my information from the students themselves. This uncertainty as to the scientific knowledge of the students was one (of many) reasons for preceding each stage of the subject-oriented courses with a common, *General Science* component.

9 Other Factors influencing Course Design

The fact that the precise language needs of the students in terms of actual reading and aural learning texts were so difficult to specify obviously created many problems for us as we began to lay down guidelines for an integrated, functionally relevant ESP course. In this particular situation, however, it may also have afforded some advantages, since it forced us to think broadly about the basic features common to different branches and modes of learning, and to make use of such humane faculties as common sense, intelligent intuition and humour. Our approach evolved from many different factors – some local, some universal. These factors included the attitudes of the students themselves to language and to learning, their relations with their teachers, the attitudes, experience and creative interests of teachers, our prior knowledge of academic theories about the nature of language teaching and scientific English, both structuralist and communicative, even the fact that there was precious little else to do in Tabriz apart from writing courses. Not least was the urgency imposed by a very limited time-scale within which the students' knowledge of English had to be activated, pointed in the right direction and brought up to a level where they could make use of advanced textbooks. But the fact that we were not bound to fixed texts or syllabuses enabled us to be more flexible in choosing materials and experimenting with teaching methods.

10 Formal and Functional Linguistic Criteria

Some of the factors affecting the development of the materials were at variance with one another. In the early stages the main conflict was between formal and functional approaches to language-teaching. At that time (1972) ideas about 'functional' and 'communicative' language-teaching and the rhetorical dimension of language use were only just beginning to filter through to Tabriz. The fact that two of us had recently studied at Edinburgh and come in contact with the ideas of H. G. Widdowson was an important influence. But most of our colleagues were still committed to structuralist, sentence-based approaches. Some structure-oriented attitudes die hard because they lend themselves to straightforward teaching methods which are satisfying in themselves even if they have little relation to how language is actually used. As we began to think out a suitable approach to teaching English in the Science Faculty, we shared

Widdowson's distrust of attempts to characterise scientific language solely by the frequency of language forms used to express it. We rejected frequency lists as a *basis* for designing a course, while recognising their potential usefulness as a means of checking the validity of our hunches about the language. We felt the need to teach the communicative value and situational use of language rather than paradigms of language forms in isolation from context.

Nevertheless, we did not wholly reject structural criteria for choosing our material because:

1 It seemed silly to throw out one approach entirely just because another had become fashionable; it was more a question of emphasis.

2 Although we could assume that the students' secondary syllabus had included the basic grammatical forms of general English, and although our attempts to remedy their deeply engrained bad language habits by drilling had not been markedly successful, this course was an introduction to the specialised language of their subjects, and we were aware that use of this language entailed a specialised grammatical competence as one aspect of an overall 'communicative competence'.[1]

3 We wanted to build productively on the previous experience and predispositions of students and teachers.

Before working out the framework of the course we prepared lists of language forms which we considered important for scientists and technologists on the grounds of frequency and usefulness. Our wish to pay special attention to the problems of mother-tongue interference were largely aborted by lack of time for the necessary research. We concentrated on those structures which we considered to create real problems of understanding, including features of discourse structure. We disregarded certain malformations which did not prevent communication. For example, some teachers became preoccupied with such quaint utterances as 'Mister, what mean this?' and exhausted their energies in trying to get the students to say 'What does this mean?' At this stage of learning, it was like water off a duck's back, and the exercise was unnecessary anyway, since it was clear what the student was trying to say. We were of course aiming mainly to teach recognition and comprehension and did not consider the production of perfect utterances to be of paramount importance provided that communication was not impeded.

The forms which we had listed were eventually linked with and subordinated to functional categories which provided the main criteria for the selection of language and round which the units of the courses were built. We tried to keep formal and functional criteria closely related in our minds at all stages in the development of the syllabus. For example, we began by excluding many social uses of language (informal suasion, expression of emotional attitudes etc.) together with such functions as narrative which were more typical of non-scientific texts; these were not likely to be encountered in academic textbooks or lectures. As a result of this decision, we concentrated mainly in our choice of verb-forms on the present tense – active and passive – together with certain modal forms associated with possibility, instructions etc.

11 Functional Basis of the Materials: Scientific Concepts

The courses which have so far been published derive from the materials which were taught to the First Year. For these introductory courses we decided to limit ourselves mainly to the language of *observation and description* – activities essential to the teaching of all branches of science and technology, although varying in importance between theoretical and applied subjects and between levels of specialisation. The Second Year materials were designed to teach the more complex or theoretical communicative activities – classification, hypothesis etc. – and their inter-relationship in the logical development of a text. For the First Year, we then sought ways of dividing up the language of description into teachable functional units. This was done by basing each unit on an important scientific concept, such as *structure*, *proportion*, *causation* etc. Not all of these are of course exclusive to the language of science and technology. Indeed, one advantage of basing our approach on such concepts was that they were readily understood by the non-scientist teacher, appealed to their intelligent curiosity about science and often revealed common ground between the latter and their own academic discipline.

The key concepts which formed the notional basis of the course were arrived at mainly intuitively from the experience of teaching scientific and technical texts for some years. We were also influenced by articles and courses produced by Pittman, Barnard, Price, Strevens and Owens.[2] None of us had any formal knowledge of scientific logic, but we did discover later that our assumptions tallied fairly closely with the analysis of R. Harre,[3] who states that 'a basic aim of science is to give adequate descriptions of systems. . . . A system has in general properties and structures . . . two kinds of description . . . can be given of a system, structure and change of state.' In fact, our course aimed to provide the learner with the means of describing the world from three viewpoints:

1 The physical state of objects, organisms etc., in terms of their properties, the location of their parts and their structure.

2 The processes which they undergo as a result of natural or human agency, including the functions of parts of a system, temporal and causal relations between events, the methods used to bring them about and the probability of their occurrence.

3 Measurement, in terms of measurable properties, quantity and proportion.

The order of development of the conceptual framework resulted from a compromise between logic and the exigencies of teaching and linguistic grading. It seemed logical to progress from static description to dynamic description via measurement, since the latter involved both physical state and human processes. But in fact treating measurement in a continuous series proved boring, so the measurement units were interspersed with those about process. Again, in dealing with the description of form which made up the first part of the course, it might have been more logical to have begun with the overall concept of structure, but we found that descriptions of structure usually contained references to properties and locations and that it was better to begin with the means of specifying these aspects, which were realised through short, simple utterances and were readily associated with certain basic grammatical items, including the use of *be* with adjectives and prepositional phrases and the use of *have* with noun phrases.

12 Cyclical Design

Our arrangement of basic concepts with associated language forms also enabled us to produce a 'cyclical' course with a cumulative learning effect. Thus Unit 1 provided ways of describing properties, Unit 2 ways of describing both the properties and location of parts of a system, Unit 3 the overall structure of a system including properties and locations; Unit 5 introduced ways of specifying the functions of parts of a system which in natural texts would often collocate with its structural description and so on. This progressive fitting together of the conceptual components of scientific description was reinforced by revision material after every three units and by the Consolidation Unit (12), in which texts could be presented showing the interplay of the conceptual components presented in previous units.

13 Advantages and Limitations of the Concept-based Approach

Our list of concepts was in no way a total inventory of the common core of scientific and technological information. Certain basic notions did not get explicit mention because they either subsumed or were subsumed by our items. For example, *behaviour* is an essential feature of many kinds of scientific description, but the idea did not generate any important language forms (not least the simple present active) which were not contained in other process units, especially that devoted to *function*. (There was some overlap of *behaviour* and *property*, which was ignored at first; later on, some reference – albeit fleeting – to dynamic properties and behavioural characteristics was included in Unit 1.) Similarly, the notion of *change* was so paramount in the description of process that it was dealt with implicitly at various stages, especially in the units about *temporal relations* and *cause and effect*.

However *ad hoc* and intuitive the means by which we arrived at our list of concepts, they provided a fertile and stimulating way of selecting and shaping the material. In addition, they afforded a useful lead-in to the teaching of the structure of discourse. They helped the learner to recognise the type of theme expressed by each part of a text, which is as important for understanding, though at a lower level, as the recognition of the rhetorical and logical organisation of the text. From a pedagogic point of view, they seemed to precede the teaching of rhetoric. Concepts formed a bridge between the scientific knowledge which the learner had already gained through his own language and the rhetorical resources by means of which this knowledge could be organised and communicated in the foreign language. We decided to begin by teaching the realisation of basic scientific concepts in English, since their meaning and relevance were easily recognisable and could be conveyed without the need for metalanguage which the overt teaching of rhetoric demanded. A notion such as *structure* seemed much more accessible to the student (and teacher) not trained in logic than an operation such as *induction*.

But we felt that a course which concentrated on the overall organisation of texts would be a logical sequel to our concept-based course.

The main advantage of using concepts as the basis for selecting our introductory material was that they encouraged language *transfer* and enabled the student to apply what he had learned to different contexts – linguistic, situational and functional. They were not tied to any particular unit of language, whether lexical, grammatical or rhetorical. Thus a notion such as causation could embrace causative verbs, types of clause and non-finite phrases, and logical connectives related to consequence and explanation. Nor were our concepts tied to topic: the concept of structure could be applied equally to the cell or the atom. Nor were they restricted to particular language functions: at the early stages of the course, our main purpose in teaching ways of specifying form and process was to enable students to make and understand descriptions; but such concepts as property, measurement, function were equally germane to the making of definitions, classifications, explanations etc., and at later stages in the course they were applied to these functions as well.

14 The Core (General Science): Content and Methodology

The aim of the course is to encourage the transfer of concepts and associated language items from one context to another. Each unit of the Core – *General Science* – presents a concept broken down into related notions (e.g. *Structure: parts and the whole/connection/composition*). The items used to realise the concept are then applied to different contexts – descriptions of objects, organisms, processes etc., sometimes explanations of states and processes. Most of these are related to science and technology in a general way; e.g. tools and laboratory equipment, chemical substances, biological processes etc. The situations chosen to exemplify and apply the concepts are very heterogeneous: the fact that we were concentrating on such basic notions enabled us to include something to appeal to all kinds of student. On the whole, the mixture of situations did not cause confusion or spark off rivalries between specialities, perhaps because the level was so general and no one branch predominated at the expense of others; mainly, however, because the relevance of the teaching points and linking concepts was self-evident. We did have trouble with certain situations for more personal reasons. For example, in an early version of a revision unit we used a bicycle extensively to bring together various notions such as structure, properties, functions, ratios (between the gears) etc. This should have been very suitable, since it was a familiar object, the outcome of the application of scientific principles to technology, and with a mechanism comprehensible to all. However, it was not popular because it was felt to be not typical of modern developed technology. So the bicycle was scrapped, with some sadness. It would probably have worked as a setting for a single item, but not as a basis for an expanded, bringing-it-all-together section.

In presenting and practising items we made use both of sets of discrete examples demonstrating the same notion (e.g. resulting changes in Unit 8, relative size in Unit 9) and single more complex situations, such as the Carbon Cycle, the parts of a car. Very often, the theme is presented through discrete examples and then applied through the description of a system, such as the plan of the town for two-dimensional shapes in Unit 1. This application may be productive – by completing descriptions, carrying out simple calculations, answering *Why?* questions about new situations using previously learned items etc., or receptive – by means of true/false questions, labelling diagrams etc. We made much use of the technique known as 'information transfer' or 'channel-conversion', whereby the student interprets diagrams, tables etc. verbally or transfers information from verbal texts into visual formats. The pedagogic advantages of this method have been stated by Widdowson:[4] it reduces the need for verbal explanation of what has to be done, promotes understanding of visual ways of displaying scientific data and vividly conveys the point that the language being learned is for use and can be applied to different contexts. The transfer of information from one *verbal* context to another is also an essential part of the learning process in the course. At its simplest, this is done on the lines of the following:

> *A book consists of pages and a cover. The pages are made of paper. A hammer consists of . . . The . . . is made of . . . and the . . .* (picture of hammer with metal head and wooden handle labelled).

The linguistic control of the 'transfer' exercises in *General Science* is fairly tight, on the assumption that the students will be discouraged if they have to flounder for words. There is, however, an open-ended aspect to many of the activities involving problem-solving, inference etc. These worked well in group-work. Even a certain amount of disagreement involved in such activities as prediction (Unit 10) could be valuable if it goaded students to 'communicate', although this could lead to chaos if taken too far. Another asset to teaching was humour. We knew that there was a relationship between successful learning and readiness to laugh, although we were also aware of the problems involved in using humorous situations, such as the difficulty of transporting them from one culture to another, and possible conflicts with the teacher's and students' views of their own roles in the classroom. On the whole, however, the students responded positively to a light-hearted approach, and one of the strongest vindications of the *General Science* course at Tabriz was that most students enjoyed doing it.

15 Differences between the Core and Specific Courses

The link between the General and specific courses was partly notional, partly linguistic. *General Science* presented the common-core language of scientific and technological description, including items of general use which were important to the scientist – e.g. *consist, depend, relationship* – and semi-technical items useful to all branches, such as dimensions and units of measurement. This aspect of the lexical content was often neglected in other EST courses, and might well constitute greater obstacles to understanding than the more obvious technical vocabulary, which was easier to learn, provided the student knew the subject. The General course also incidentally presented many of the common ways of presenting information visually. The Core course was mainly limited to single utterances or very brief texts, except in the revision units. The specific courses were aimed at the understanding of extended texts, within the domain of the relevant disciplines. Each specific unit opened with a section which presented some of the general items from the Core in the context of topics drawn from the subject. At this stage associated specialised language items were introduced and linked with the general items where appropriate. This would involve making more delicate lexical distinctions than those in the General unit and pointing out exponents of the concepts whose use was specific to the subject; sometimes the same item would be shown to have different meanings or shades of meaning in general and specialised usage. The techniques of presentation and practice in the opening of the specific units are similar to the exercises in *General Science*. These sections have been expanded in the published versions to make it possible to use the specific courses independently of the General course, with more advanced classes.

16 Problems in Designing Specific Courses and Linking Them with the Core

As the specific courses developed, and as our knowledge of the subjects deepened, they tended to become more advanced in content. *General Science* concentrated on the basic language and concepts common to all disciplines and did not pretend to reflect the level of knowledge of university entrants. As we came to apply the concepts to the student's own subject, however, it became increasingly necessary to relate the themes to his background knowledge. Various important problems arose, which may be faced by anyone attempting to develop an ESP syllabus which relates the student's linguistic and study needs to his subject needs, especially if the writer is not a scientist:

1 We had to consider whether the range of topics chosen reflected a reasonable coverage of the different aspects of the subject. This was particularly difficult in a branching subject such as Engineering.

2 On the other hand, it was desirable that the course should have a thematic unity, and not just be a mixture of topics, either by having individual units or sections devoted to particular subjects, or by systematically recycling themes and contexts. Satisfying these criteria while following our notional syllabus proved to be quite a tricky balancing act.

3 There were many advantages in having a common notional/linguistic framework for different courses. This was not just an aid to coordinating the writing and teaching: it provided the student and teacher with recognisable language-learning aims and landmarks through the course, and ensured that non-scientists concentrated on the language and study needs rather than ending up trying to teach the subject *per se*. On the other hand, we had to maintain a very flexible attitude to the broad functional categories we were dealing with. Obviously we had to make compromises with the realities of the subject. Sometimes it was difficult to reconcile our order of concepts with the priorities or pedagogic sequences of the subject. Similar problems are no doubt faced in designing a course based on rhetorical criteria. On the other hand, I think that our concepts – related to Form, Process and Measurement – were sufficiently basic to be fairly central to all subjects. Seeking relationships between concept and subject forced us to increase our understanding of both. For example, in looking for topics to

exemplify the notion of Property in Biology and Engineering, it was no good throwing together random descriptions of materials or organisms: we had to consider *why* a biologist or an engineer was interested in Property: what were the relevant contexts to which he would apply the concept? As a result of these enquiries, the applicability of the concept broadened out into the classification of organisms in Biology and the technological uses of materials in Engineering; these were topics important to the subjects, the comprehension of which depended on the concept of Property.

4 The greatest problem has probably been that of level of specialisation. Initially, we relied a good deal on fairly elementary textbooks or works of popular science which presented the information we sought simply, often with graphic illustrations which could be adapted for 'information transfer' exercises. However, we were gradually awakened (with the aid of scientist advisers) to the fact that this information was not only simplified, often it was actually 'wrong' in the light of more advanced and precise study; an example is the way the conception, description and pictorialisation of electron changes at different stages in learning.[5] We are forced by the student's linguistic limitations and the teacher's lack of knowledge to stick to a fairly low level, which has meant including statements and descriptions which may be acceptable from a language-learning point of view but are at least inadequate from an academic point of view.

17 The Approach to Discourse

Another way in which our approach to the specific books has been modified in the course of their development has been in the treatment of discourse. As it was originally conceived, the course aimed to concentrate on relatively brief utterances and texts exemplifying various concepts which would prepare students to deal with the organisation of longer texts later. However, as the reading and listening exercises in the specific books were developed, we found it increasingly necessary and useful to include activities which practised skills essential for the understanding of continuous texts. This has been done on a fairly informal basis, on the assumption that the course will be followed by types of learning devoted specifically to rhetoric and reading strategies. It has included the application of other kinds of 'rhetorical act' apart from description – e.g. classification, comparison, induction (not necessarily overt), prediction; inference exercises practising the logical consequences of parts of a text, through which the student applies information gained from reading or listening to *Why?/How do you know?* questions; exercises drawing attention to the use of cohesive devices, the outline of texts and their order of development.[6]

18 Nucleus and Wider Developments in ESP

Although our approach to ESP was conceived and born in a rugged environment, remote from both the world of academic theory and the world of publishing, we have since had the opportunity to view it in perspective, as part of the energetic experimentation and debate which is now going on in the field of English for Specific Purposes, and which will be reflected within the covers of this book. The debate has two directions – one divergent, with the emphasis on the word 'specific', the other convergent, seeking common factors and policies. On the one hand, there is a growing awareness of the many different variables embraced by the term ESP. These include the geographic, sociolinguistic and academic setting for the teaching of English; what other ways – if any – English is used outside the language-class; the cultural, linguistic and educational experience, expectations, prejudices of students and teachers; the types of language and study skill needed; the level and area of study and degree of motivation; teaching conditions and equipment; availability of textbooks and access to specialist knowledge etc. In recent years a distinction has emerged – itself pretty rough – between 'academic' and 'occupational' language needs. In Britain there has been an increasing interest – coinciding with academic developments in discourse analysis – in courses for foreign students and trainees in an English-speaking environment, whose language needs include the ability to survive socially and to communicate in a greater variety of situations than would be the case in their own country. In many cases they are also more motivated and specialised in their subject. These situations have generated an interest in teaching methods directed towards study skills, the use of 'authentic materials' and individualised learning; these methods are certainly desirable as target activities even in a situation like Tabriz, but they are of limited practicality at the initial stages of learning, for students with little knowledge of English and still less opportunity to practise it, low or vague motivation, patchy knowledge of their subject and no familiarity with or strong resistance to self-teaching techniques.

The search for factors common to these multifarious learning situations is also, I think, desirable – especially where the aim is the discovery of shared categories and patterns of communication and information structure, or the development of closer understanding and collaboration between the scientist and the language-teacher.

Nucleus was itself a compromise between a number of quite diverse factors – academic, linguistic, pedagogic, geographic, personal. Some of these factors were unique to that situation, but it seems that the kind of compromise underlying the approach may be applicable to other, very different situations.

REFERENCES

1 This point is developed by Keith Johnson: 'The Production of Functional Materials and their Integration within Existing Language-Teaching Programmes', *ELT Documents*, 1976/1; British Council ETIC.
2 Pittman, G. A., 'Trade and Technical English', *ELT* II, pp. 39–46.
   Barnard, Helen, *Advanced English Vocabulary*, Newbury House, 1971.
   Owens, G. T., *English Words and Structures in Science and Maths*, Singapore, 1970.
   Price, R. F., *A Reference Book of English Words and Phrases for Foreign Science Students*, Pergamon Press, 1966.
   Strevens, P. D., 'Technological and Scientific English', *ELT* XXVII.
3 Harré, R., *An Introduction to the Logic of the Sciences*, Macmillan, 1967, pp. 48–49.
4 Widdowson, H. G., 'Two Types of Communicative Exercise', AILA/BAAL Seminar, Lancaster, 1973.
5 I am grateful to Arthur Godman, Science Adviser to the Series, for this example and much other advice on the teaching of Science.
6 There are many examples of such exercises in the later units of *Nucleus: Biology*. Some have been described by Donald Adamson in ESPMENA (Khartoum) No. 4.

PART THREE

Case Studies: Syllabi and Materials

We move now to five Case Studies of situations in which syllabi and materials have been designed to teach English for a specific purpose. A common factor in each case is that the students are postgraduates from overseas, studying for diplomas and masters degrees at British Universities – Newcastle, Manchester and Lancaster. The subject areas they are studying range from Soil Science (Ch. 7), Forestry and Agriculture (Ch. 8), Economics (Ch. 9), to Engineering, Economics and Urban Planning (Ch. 10). Three of the Case Studies, Chapters 8, 9 and 10, focus sharply on listening skills required to understand lectures, together with note-taking (particularly Chs. 9 and 10). All five studies are concerned, to a greater or lesser extent, with the problem of making students aware of the structure and organisation of English above the sentence level – of contextual and pragmatic meaning (Ch. 10), or the expository procedures or techniques used in discourse.

Thus, we can describe the special purpose of learning English for these students as one of survival – *academically* in their professional studies, and *socially* in and around the University. (This is the particular concern of the syllabus and materials described in Chapter 6.) The fact that each of these studies is concerned with teaching English to overseas students in England rather than overseas, should not detract from the direct relevance of each of them to similar situations abroad. Essentially the same situations exist where students are about to enter tertiary level education, particularly if English is to be the medium of instruction. Of course, in many cases, the students' level of English proficiency is much lower. In most universities in developing countries a certain amount of lecture instruction takes place in English, either from expatriate lecturers, or by L_1 lecturers recently returned from Britain or the United States. In nearly all situations students are required to read notes or textbooks in English at some stage in their course; in many countries final degree examinations are written in English. Thus, in many cases failure to learn English – or, to put it more precisely, failure to cope adequately with spoken instruction or written texts in English – leads to educational failure at the University. In the case of overseas postgraduate students at British Universities such failure can be costly, as well as humiliating and depressing for the individual concerned.

The aims, and the materials to meet these aims, described in Chapters 7, 8 and 9 form the substance of what has come to be known as *Study Skills*, which are explicitly the concern of the programme described in Chapter 10. The notion of Study Skills is particularly useful for at least three reasons: (a) it is a skills-integrating notion – 'any one "study situation" requires more than one "linguistic skill" (Ch. 10, 3.3)'; (b) it automatically leads to concern with inter-sentential features such as information structuring and discourse relationships; and (c) it focusses attention on the skills involved in studying in a foreign language at University, which in most cases are significantly different from students previous learning and study habits (even, it should be added, during previous undergraduate University experience). Unfortunately, too little is known about *studying* as a psycho- and sociolinguistic phenomena. Many EST courses in developing countries aim to teach study skills without any very clear information about study methods currently employed, or how they relate to, or conflict with, those being taught.

Finally, we would like to think that all the contributors to (and readers of) this book echo the sentiment expressed by Straker Cook in Chapter 6.

> 'My concern is simply to pay something more than lipservice to *language use*, and to try not to produce that common phenomenon, the learner who "drills beautifully" in the classroom, but who remain essentially inarticulate outside it.'

The approaches to syllabi and materials in Parts II and III are all broadly similar in that they are renewed attempts to teach not just English language but Communication Skills in English. Such attempts arise not only from the growing requirements for specialised language instruction at the tertiary level, but also from a disatisfaction with turning out merely 'well-drilled students'; for these requirements have led to a concern with the notion of communication competence, while the disatisfaction has led to a corresponding shift in attention towards understanding and creating discourse.

6

A 'Social Survival' Syllabus

R. STRAKER COOK

1 Rationale of the Syllabus

1.1 *Place of the Syllabus in a Unified Scheme*

The outline syllabus presented here was designed to serve as the first part of a remedial English course for overseas postgraduate students at the University of Newcastle upon Tyne. The course was to be based on a unified syllabus in which optional materials practising the use of English in various disciplines (Parts II and III) branched out from a 'spine' or common-core element (Part I). The total scheme is based on exposition and practice of the procedures involved in organising and expressing scientific and other specialised information.

The function of the spine is introductory and unifying. Its content is 'neutral' with respect to a particular student's particular discipline, but the procedures used in specialist English clearly relate to communicative acts in everyday situations and find their expression (though no doubt somewhat elliptically and unsystematically) in colloquial English. Each unit in the spine introduces a procedure ('defining', for example) as exemplified in everyday situations and non-specialist English use. The settings and dialogues are based on the general theme of adjusting to student life in a British university, and by focussing on such practicalities as arranging timetables, finding accommodation and so on, they provide some means of social survival. When students have worked through the unit they proceed to a corresponding unit in Part II, which would practise 'defining' in specialist use, with emphasis on reading and writing skills: then they move to a corresponding unit in Part III, again instancing 'defining' but concentrating on aural comprehension and oral production in such 'academic situations' as lectures, seminars, practical work. Parts II and III would provide optional materials to illustrate 'defining' in texts and tape recordings from a range of disciplines, to suit the speciality of individual students or small groups of students. The three parts are therefore used conjointly, and the students work through the units in the following pattern:

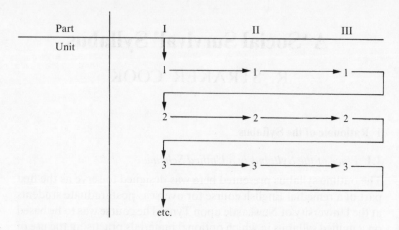

In this way, the three parts each constitute a self-contained syllabus, and could if required be used separately: placed together and worked through in the proper sequence, they represent a unified syllabus.

1.2 *General Orientation of the Syllabus*

The procedures which were to be covered by the unified scheme were: definition; classification (as a basis for identification and ordering of data, and for making value judgements); description of properties, of processes or operations, of their consequences, and of states; the use of these procedures in discussion of hypothetical situations and in the delineation of the conditions under which a rule or statement applies. However, the degree to which one is aware of using such procedures in the act of communicating, and the extent to which they are explicitly expressed, constitutes one of the principal differences between everyday and specialised language use. Shifts in the degree of awareness/explicitness can be traced through several types of discourse which we will characterise as 'formal written', 'discussive' and 'conversational'. The first and third are self-explanatory: the third denotes spoken discussion of specialised topics, and so characterises the use of English in discussion groups and in 'unread' or informally-presented lectures.

As an example of such shifts, one may under ordinary circumstances list a number of items in the course of conversation but would probably not mark them as being listed or ordered: in discussion of a specialised topic one would be much more likely to mark them with expressions of ordinality such as 'first/firstly; second/secondly' but one would quite probably do so inconsistently, and tend to abandon this marking after 'thirdly' or perhaps 'fourthly': it is very unlikely that one would resort to sub-lists. In written English on a specialised topic listing would be virtually obligatory: it would be systematic, might well contain sub-lists, and would probably resort either to more elaborate phraseology ('in the fourth place ...', 'in the fifth instance ...', 'our sixth consideration ...') or above all to a system of symbols (numerals – Roman and Arabic: letters – Roman and Greek, etc.) in conjunction with systematic tabulation. To take a further instance: a casual enquiry on the street eliciting confirmation or clarification would merit some introductory phrase as, 'Please can you tell me (if this is the way to ...)', or 'This *is* (the way to) ..., isn't it?' In a discussive setting the enquiry might be introduced by 'Would I be/Am I right in thinking that ...'. In specialist writing such an introduction would be depersonalised by use of the plural or an impersonal construction, would in all probability signal a greater caution or reserve and would take account of the absence of an addressee – 'We might be justified in supposing that ...' 'From this it might be inferred that ...'. Our syllabus has therefore to meet two requirements of organisation: the first is to establish in everyday situations and language the use of procedures which are elaborated in a more overt and conscious manner in specialised English. The second is to move from informal to semi-formal realisations, and from informal to semi-formal situations.

These requirements carry several implications for the general shape of the syllabus. If we order our materials in terms of such procedures as definition, comparison, classification, description of states, of properties, of processes, and so on, then a linear grading of structural features will not be possible since many such features will recur for different procedures. Further, some procedures are subsumed by others – comparison is, for example, a prior procedure to classification, and will be implied in any exemplification of the latter. It follows that once presented, the procedures (and associated structural features) will be constantly reincorporated in subsequent units of the syllabus. In this sense the syllabus is necessarily spiral in nature. Since our primary interest is in the exemplification and manipulation of procedures, rather than the structures which they incorporate, we will be concerned very largely with relationships extending beyond the sentence: and since we intend to relate these procedures to everyday situations, we will be concerned with stretches of discourse rather than with isolated sentences.

1.3   *A Situation-Based Syllabus*

This preoccupation with situations and with stretches of dialogue-format discourse was somewhat novel when the syllabus was first planned in 1971. It coincided with the appearance of a number of articles reappraising the value of structural drills and suggesting that a situational approach might offer more relevant practice (some are listed at the end of this chapter). While it is pleasing to see that the situational approach has since gained wider recognition (Wilkins, 1972, Council for Cultural Cooperation, 1973, Widdowson, 1973 (Chapter 10)) it must be borne in mind that there are certain inherent difficulties which still need to be resolved. The most obvious is that 'raw' situations as they are encountered in everyday life cannot directly form the basis of teaching materials – they are too closely tied to particular circumstances, and would offer no more than a series of random exchanges. Secondly there is a danger that in concentrating on the creation of appropriate and realistic dialogues we may lose sight of formal language priorities. Thirdly, since the use of 'situations' in the classroom is by no means new, there is little point in redefining the situational approach and giving it new vigour, if appropriate methods of presentation and teaching are not evolved to gain full benefit from the reorientation of syllabus and materials.

The outline syllabus and specimen materials appended here were an attempt to answer three questions: Can a situation-based syllabus be endowed with an overall structural cohesion? Can 'teaching through situations' be given a fresh methodological significance? Can realistic dialogues be created without loss of structural control? It seems to me that the solutions proposed are still relevant and merit further development and application.

1.4   *Structure of the Syllabus*

Let us start on the basis that a procedure such as 'defining' employs one of a limited set of logical relationships. Each of these relationships may be expressed in several different ways depending on such factors as the formality of the occasion, who is addressing whom, what effect the speaker wishes to create. This provides a set of alternative structural patterns for the expression of each logical relationship, though we can, of course, place limits on the number of logical relationships and expressional variants in the syllabus.

Furthermore, each procedure suggests a set of situations which typically require its use and this fact is exploited in the syllabus structure given diagrammatically, unit by unit, on pages 109 to 111. Each unit is derived from the *axis* of organisation of the unified syllabus: thus under 'axis' in Unit 3 we have selected the same procedures – description of properties, the phrases of a process, the use of relatives – which appear in Unit 3 of Part II of the syllabus, where they are developed in relation to specialised uses of English. These procedures provide a structural *framework* for dialogues or narrative, and suggest a suitable *theme* for the production of a number of very short *episodes* which illustrate and practice the use of the coordinating features in everyday situations. From Unit 3 onwards the theme is also developed in the form of *texts* which are instances of the informal presentation of topics of general interest. This arrangement, it seems to me, gives the kind of cohesion which a situation-based syllabus would require: cohesion of grammatical patterns is ensured by the fact that each episode is derived from the same structural framework: situational cohesion is ensured because each episode develops the same theme under varying circumstances.

We also satisfy several other conditions which a situational approach would seem to require: we supply new formal patterns in a format which enables the student to extend language use directly from his first language; this the structural drill was never able to do, since it denied the very connection between language form and situation on which the student must build. We replace a succession of structural examples by a controlled and ordered succession of situational examples. And to practice these examples, we replace the structural drill by the *situation-routine* which is described below.

Textual length and manner of presentation are given particular attention. The episodes are kept as short as credibility and naturalness will allow, especially in the first two units, and they are intensively practised as complete instances of form and use. Clearly, sentences will not of themselves serve as the basis for this work, and equal weight must be given to a structural framework and to appropriate thematic settings. (Yet this will, paradoxically, permit us to teach incomplete sentences: it has always seemed odd to me that such a common feature of the spoken language should be so carefully avoided, while many idioms receive undue attention. Students often find it difficult to locate the referential 'root' of an incomplete sentence and their English is marked by an inability to formulate incomplete sentences in a natural way. I do not wish to labour the point unduly, but it would be borne in mind in creating the dialogues.)

At first the distinction between episode and situation may seem trivial: it is however essential to this syllabus. The same short episode may often be repeated, with a few modifications, in a similar situation. Consultation of the diagram for Unit 2 will illustrate this. Selection is a common theme in everyday exchanges, and the underlying procedure is one of classification: we illustrate the theme with two short episodes – purchasing something, and joining a University society. But purchases are common and varied, and the same episode may recur at the grocers, at the shoe shop, at the car showroom and so on. This is indicated by the fact that 'purchases' is branched into *two* illustrative episodes – 'eggs' and 'shoes'. Selection would not be complete, however, without some kind of evaluation, underlying which are sequential and comparative procedures.* So a second theme is developed, and illustrated from the same type of episode: this time the dialogues emphasise not so much a choice as the reasons for that choice. The episodes, because they can be reapplied to a number of similar situations, may be multiplied to provide supplementary practice. Equally, I envisage the inclusion of optional materials developed in this manner, and I wish to emphasise the freedom of the teacher or instructor to devise his own episodes where he feels the need to. The open-endedness of the episodes is diagrammatically represented in Unit 3 by the unlabelled branches – in principle any of the episodes in any of the units are expandable in the same way, though some may prove more fruitful than others.

A last consideration is the broad setting of the episodes. As already stated, the 'spine' is intended to develop the University and academic life as the general setting for its materials. This is applied with varying degrees of superficiality: episodes ii and iv of Unit 2, ia and ib of Unit 4, iv of Unit 5, are closely tied to University activities; so also are all but one of the texts. More superficially all episodes of Unit 1, at least some of the alternatives at i and ii, Unit 3, iia and iib of Unit 4, and ii and iii of Unit 5, are to be given a University setting simply by the people and locations we choose to insert. Even more superficially, iiia

---

* This is no less true of the specialised use of English, and the same procedures are to be seen at work in Unit 2 of Part II of the syllabus, to which students progress from Unit 2 of this syllabus. It is in this way that selection of an *axis* provides an overstructure for the unified scheme.

and b can be set in the University student travel office, and the second text of Unit 5 might describe an incident at a student dance. In other instances we step outside the academic sphere simply to avoid monotony.

1.5 *The Use of 'Situations' in Class*

Let us consider next what 'teaching through situations' and the use of situations in the classroom may imply. Firstly, 'contextualisation' has in the past tended to consist of no more than a couple of supplementary sentences acting as a 'frame' for the key sentence. The frame is itself divorced from context in a broader sense: it is not actualised in a way which will impinge upon the student's own interests and motivation and so render the contextualisation truly meaningful. Secondly, 'situational' teaching is often taken to mean no more than the supply of actions or illustrations in the classroom – jumping, making students open doors, placing the inevitable pen on the ever-available book. These are, I would say, entirely artificial and induced activities. While not wishing to discredit them altogether – they have their limited value – they hardly merit the term situational; and if we do not go on to relate them to actual situations their value is very limited indeed. A first step is to liberate situational teaching from the confines of strict structural grading, and one hopes that this scheme will provide sufficient flexibility without a loss of control over structural presentation. But I feel that far greater artificiality is produced by lexical than by structural grading, and I would like to introduce the idea of expendable items. Having selected, on whatever basis, the lexical items one wishes the learner to retain as a part of his repertory, I see no harm in introducing a few expendable items to enhance the realism of a dialogue or text. In subsequent practice and in later stages of the course they might be dropped altogether. Used judiciously and sparingly, this tactic in no way introduces haphazard elements, if one thinks in terms of naturalness of situation. In terms of learning economy, one has to offset a certain lexical redundancy against the learning value of realistic and meaningful situations.

A second step is to ensure that situations are not reduced to locative stereotypes such as 'At the Butchers', with little beyond lexical items from the appropriate register to distinguish them from other 'situations'. This can be achieved by concentrating on the dynamic aspects of the situation: who are the participants, what do they wish to say, what communicative acts are involved? The third step is to a methodological one. Communicative fluency is established by intensive repetition and practice of the *dialogue build-up*, which is a drill, to be sure, but a communicative rather than a structural one: it leads into rehearsal and acting out of the full dialogue, and the entire sequence of practice is referred to as a situation-routine.

What we present, then, are controlled situations which retain as much of the flavour of real-life situations as possible: and we enhance the sense of realism by practising situation-routines. Nothing, of course can overcome the in-built artificiality of the *teaching* situation itself, and this is the pitfall of the earlier 'situational method'. My concern is simply to pay something more than lip-service to *language use*, and to try not to produce that common phenomenon, the learner who 'drills beautifully' in the classroom and remains essentially inarticulate outside it. I must admit that the programmes with which I have been associated over the last few years have tended, despite intentions to the contrary, to turn out well-drilled students.

1.6 *Providing Realistic Dialogues*

There remains the question of a procedure for the creation of dialogues. How are we to strike a balance between realism and control? James (1970) suggests giving a topic of discussion to twenty pairs of subjects and collating and condensing the results of each discussion. But the whole procedure smacks of artificiality – from selection of topic to behaviour of subjects under abnormal circumstances, to the subjectiveness of the collation procedure. The method I would wish to use is as follows: a subject is chosen and without any briefing is asked to perform a verbal task under 'real' conditions – e.g. to ask his way to a certain address, to make a business appointment, or to get into a conversation with a stranger, on a bus say, and bring the conversation round to a given topic. The course planner accompanies without participation: he records the exchange and prepares a tapescript. The same tasks and conditions are repeated with several subjects. We can then create a single dialogue on the basis of compared tapescripts. This is still a subjective business, of course, but there is less risk of artificiality, and haphazard content is avoided because the dialogue must fit a pre-determined framework. So a two-way process ensues: the exchanges are modified sufficiently, but minimally, to accommodate them to the framework, and at the same time the framework is modified, or its link with a given theme is modified, wherever actual usage diverges markedly from our preconceptions about the dialogue.

The resulting balance should produce highly realistic dialogues without the dangers of what James calls 'random exchanges'. A procedure this elaborate could not, of course, be adopted for the materials sketched out here. The dialogues are purely imagined and the frameworks are entirely unmodified: they should be taken merely as illustrating the function that more carefully-devised frameworks and dialogues would fulfil in the structure of this syllabus.

2 The Syllabus

2.1 *Preliminary Note on Grading and Syllabus Layout*

(i) The object of the exercise has been to grade episodes, starting from a particular procedure, or combination of procedures, and exploiting the themes which these suggest. In the unitary layouts the design is given by branching lines. Thus in Unit 5 'Hypothesis' produces, as a theme, discussion of a conjectural nature, this being illustrated by the first two texts, of which one is on a fairly restricted topic, the other on a topic of more general interest. 'Operations' divides into mechanical operations and physical-mental operations. The two procedures in combination provide the theme of hypothetical operations – as when one makes conjectures about operations that are uncertain, or about events which may have resulted from one of several operations.

(ii) *Structural grading* is consequential upon situational grading. While it is for this reason not haphazard, it could not be exactly specified unless the entire set of dialogues and texts (i.e. virtually the entire course) were written out in full. Features which would receive particular emphasis are given in the notes on each unit. A very approximate grading of sentence complexity is intended, in that internal dependencies (as also intersentential dependencies) are to be kept as simple as possible without loss of verisimilitude in the first two units, and more complex interdependencies freely allowed in later units.

(iii) *Lexical grading* is also unspecified, though this is not to say that it is undirected. On the one hand, it is impossible to predict which items will be new, or present special difficulties, for a given student – this being a remedial course for students from varied backgrounds. Also the inventive role of the teacher, which we encourage, makes specification difficult. On the other hand, we and the teacher are working within a brief, which is (a) to concentrate on aspects of University life and academic activities. and (b), to treat as expendable any items introduced in the interests of realism but not considered to be of immediate utility. The *rate* of lexical presentation will be fairly even. The number of items which may be unfamiliar to most students will be fairly high in Unit 1; on the other hand, each unit contains somewhat more material than the preceding one, so that despite re-use of items, the introduction of items which are 'new' to the body of materials should be more or less constant.

2.2 *Layout of the Syllabus*

See pages 109–111.

3 Presentation and Teaching Method

3.1 *General Presentation*

(i) The syllabus consists virtually of teaching notes together with the requisite materials: the students will only need cyclostyled copies of the dialogues and texts and possibly copies of some of the illustrations. However, it is recommended that the dialogues be reproduced in the same format as the one adopted here.

(ii) Particular care is required in presentation and handling of the dialogues. The following steps are envisaged:

1 Read the text several times – normal conversational speed; take care not to be too 'careful' in enunciation; try to maintain consistent and natural intonation.

2 Hand out copies of text; students are unlikely to have met an entirely oral presentation and will be more at home with the text in their hands. Discuss difficulties, lexical or other, students may have; explain situation, implications, overtones, textual signals of tensions between personae. From Unit 2 onwards, the longer dialogues may be used as the basis for aural comprehension exercises.

3 Without text, practise sectional repetition, in chorus. Use the expansions given under the heading 'Dialogue Build-up'. Practise until students are able to repeat fluently and naturally. They need not memorise the dialogue, though this may be an advantage with the shorter ones. *Important:* remember that

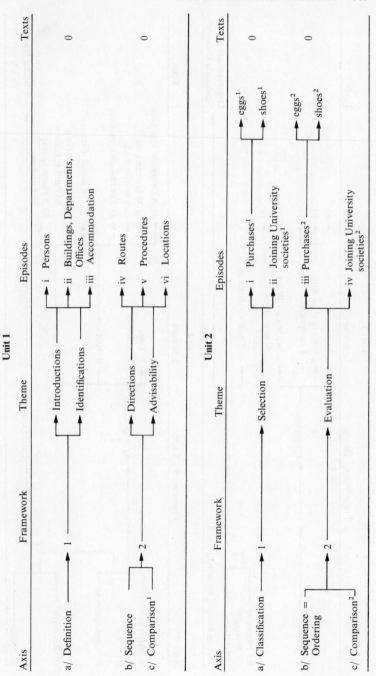

Unit 1

Axis	Framework	Theme	Episodes	Texts
a/ Definition → 1		Introductions	i Persons	0
			ii Buildings, Departments, Offices	
		Identifications	iii Accommodation	
b/ Sequence	2	Directions	iv Routes	0
c/ Comparison[1]			v Procedures	
		Advisability	vi Locations	

Unit 2

Axis	Framework	Theme	Episodes	Texts
a/ Classification → 1		Selection	i Purchases[1]	eggs[1] shoes[1]
			ii Joining University societies[1]	0
b/ Sequence = Ordering	2	Evaluation	iii Purchases[2]	eggs[2] shoes[2]
c/ Comparison[2]			iv Joining University societies[2]	0

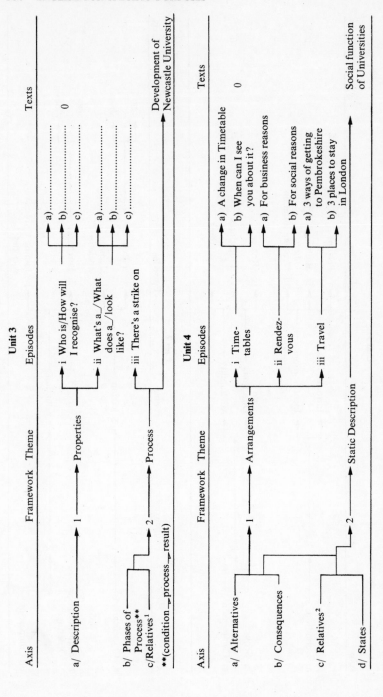

Unit 5

Axis	Framework	Theme	Episodes	Texts
a/ Hypothesis	1	Conjectural discussion		Future role of Universities
	2	Mechanical	i Cigarette machine	
			ii The lift's stuck	
				Implications of an improbable situation
		Physical-mental	iii Using a cricket bat	
			iv Preparing a report	
b/ Operations	3	Hypothetical operation		Working a gadget-laden tape-recorder
				incorporating revisional materials

the phrases in the Dialogue Build-up are, or are converted into, fragments of the dialogue; they should not be treated as if they really stood alone. This is especially true of intonation and stress patterns. Take for example Unit 1, Episode (ii), Situation (b): this contains the phrase 'come in here', which appears as No. 3 in the Build-up. In isolation the most probable stress position would be 'come in here': it is essential to maintain the *dialogue* stress position as the sentence is built up. Look at Unit 1, Episode (i), Situation (b), Nos. 14 and 15 of the Build-up, for a further example: to make quite clear the distinction carried by the stress position, we also give the more frequent pattern.

4 After a little practice with the entire dialogue, use groups to act out the dialogue turn by turn: insist on rapidity and fluency, and act virtually as a *producer*, demanding movement, facial expression, as far as natural gifts of individual students will allow: draw attention to typically 'foreign' gestures, show link with foreign stress pattern if this is also present. Students should have the texts to hand, but should not read out the parts; they are to be used for 'rescue' purposes only.

5 From Unit 3 onwards, follow active practice with limited discussion of reductions and simplifications in informal speech: illustrate and practise by dialogue recapitulation.

6 Discuss situations of a similar type which students themselves have encountered, ask what difficulties they had; help them to build up, in group work, parallel dialogues which will fit these situations.

3.2 *Notes on the Presentation of Individual Units*

UNIT 1

Features of Organisation

1 Dialogue practice is enhanced by the fact that certain dialogues have been given a very close superficial resemblance. Consequently they have shared structural and idiomatic features, the patterns of recurrence being as follows:

This recurrence would, of course, be a feature of subsequent units when written in full detail.

2 In spoken exchanges the requesting of definitions probably features almost as prominently as the giving of definitions. This unit covers, beyond expansions and variants of the standard definition forms, the following patterns of definition-requests:

what/where/who/which/ + BE + N/Pron. (with expansions)
show/tell, etc. (with expansions) + *me,* etc. + *which,* etc. (+ BE) + N
(with expansions) (+ BE)

3 Sequence links exploited are:

first . . ./then . . ./and . . ./until . . . :
also lexico-semantic links, e.g. *take* it to them . . . → they will *give*

4 Comparison: -er -est forms: intersentential comparisons: implied comparisons, e.g. main lecture room *vs.* seminar room/'will it take long?' *vs.* 'there's quite a queue'.

UNIT 2

Features of Organisation

1 Classification using
   (i) BE, HAVE, STOCK, etc. + sorts/kinds/types, etc.
   (ii) adjective + N/one(s)/adj. -e.g. brown eggs; white ones; brown, white.
   (iii) Numeral + sorts, etc. + 'for example . . .'/'such as . . .'

2 Ordering and Comparison using mixed ordinals, prepositions and comparatives. e.g. 'best of all . . .'/'second . . .'/'then . . .'/'worst . . .'. Emphasis on 'irregular' formation of comparatives.

UNIT 3

Features of Organisation

Descriptive strategies based on: HAVE/HAVE + got / BE / agent-less passive forms.

Phases of process/relatives: conditions introduced through relative + BE: results introduced through relative + Vb.: reduced relatives using -ing forms.

Stylistic contrasts between episode (iii) and the text:

Episode (iii): Agent expressed as 'they, we, you'. Lexical items to include 'so, because of/outcome, upshot'. Inexact time expressions: 'a couple of years back/about three months ago'.

The text: Impersonal, passive constructions: agent unexpressed. Lexical items to include 'consequently, due to/result, effect'. 'Exact time expressions: '1833, 1937, 1st August 1963'.

Presentation: Not only do Episodes (i) and (ii) lend themselves to exploitation, but straight description often seems to require considerable practice. From a set of readily-constructed situations we proceed to short exercises in description. One of the students can sit in front of the group, which then attempts to describe him accurately: various objects, present or absent, may be essayed. End up with a couple of 'problems' e.g. a pair of curling tongs, a surrealist or abstract painting. Episode (iii) should be followed up with a short aural comprehension exercise, and with discussion of a current or recent strike. The text – and all subsequent texts – will be followed by aural comprehension.

UNIT 4

Features of Organisation
Alternatives and consequences expressed by 'supposing . . .'/'instead of . . .'/'the one hand . . ., the other (hand)'. 'If'-clauses: 'if . . ., (then) . . .' and '. . ., if . . .' 'if'-clause + Q form: Q-form + 'of'-clause. Possibility introduced by 'would', 'could'. Expressions of future time: combined time-and-place expressions, e.g. 'on . . . at . . . in/ at . . .'.

Reintroduction of relatives from Unit 3 with further reduced forms. \
States expressed through s. pres. tense } in combination with alternatives/consequences

Presentation: The situations selected here offer good scope for dialogue applications. (i) (a) can be followed up by use of students' actual timetables and the insertion of an imaginary new course of a given number of hours per week. Episode (ii) could be the occasion for practice in using the telephone, (a) because such arrangements are commonly made by telephone, (b) because foreign learners find it so hard to conduct a telephone conversation, (c) because (and quite incidentally to our main intention) the 'phone makes a learner aware, to an even greater extent than does the language laboratory, of the communicative shortcomings of his 'transitional' phonetic/prosodic abilities. Episode (iii) can be supported by maps, rail/air schedules, hotel and boarding house adverts, a street map of London, and so on.

UNIT 5

Features of Organisation
I suggested earlier that some procedures appear to subsume others (p. 101) and this is particularly true of hypothesising, which may incorporate techniques of definition, of sequence, consequence, phases of process, and so on. It is therefore particularly valuable for the revisional presentation of materials (as indicated diagrammatically on p. 111). 'Operations' is not, strictly speaking, a procedure of organisation; however, it has considerable revisional value in that operational description incorporates sequencing, classification, and processual phases. (Indeed, that same combination of procedures is to be found in the fifth unit of Part II of the General Syllabus.) We have mentioned the opportunities for conjectural discussion provided by combining these in turn with hypothesising.

Presentation: Episodes (i), (ii), (iv) in particular will produce longish dialogues requiring careful presentation. The dialogues are, in effect, a distillation from extended exchanges in real life. I suggest there is a point at which one should abandon the formality of the dialogue routine for the kind of informal discussion we have been nursing through previous units (see the notes on presentation above, and the dialogue applications illustrated below). It seems convenient to fix this at the stage where procedural complexity has been introduced and where continued use of formal presentation will only be possible with large concessions in verisimilitude. Consequently, we provide two texts – the last two – with plentiful possibilities for extended, informal, anecdotal discussion. The teacher's new role is to give mild guidance and sparing corrections: the student should be ready by now for the semi-independent work which, we envisage, would follow on from this syllabus.

4 A Provisional Version of Unit 1

4.1 *Suggested Materials for Episode (i)*

SITUATION (A)

Juan, who has just arrived at the University is walking down the road with Ben, who is in his second year:

BEN   JUAN

See that man over there?
He's Mr Pearson.

                                           Who's he?

He's a lecturer in the Physics
Department.

                                           Will he lecture to us at all?

No, he's the bloke who arranges
our timetables.

Dialogue Build-up

 1 See that man over there?   9 Will he lecture?
 2 He's Mr Pearson   10 will he lecture to us?
 3 Who's he?   11 will he lecture to us at all?
 4 He's a lecturer   12 No
 5 Physics Department   13 our timetables
 6 in the Physics Department   14 he arranges our timetables
 7 he's in the Physics Depart-   15 he's the bloke who arranges
    ment   our timetables
 8 he's a lecturer in the Physics
    Department

SITUATION (B)

Mr Pearson, who is in charge of foreign students, has arranged a
party to introduce new students to some of the staff:

MR PEARSON   JUAN   JOHN HARRINGTON

Juan, this is John
Harrington.

                                           Pleased to meet you,
                                           Mr er . . .

                        Mendoza, Juan
                        Mendoza. I'm in the
                        Department of
                        Agriculture. What
                        are you studying?

                                           Oh, I'm not. I'm,
                                           well, Professor
                                           Harrington.
                                           Professor of
                                           Engineering. Are
                                           you in your first year
                                           Mr er . . . ?

Mendoza. Yes and no. You see, I'm a research student. I've just arrived here.

He's expecting to do something in agricultural engineering. Isn't that right?

Well well, we seem to have something in common, Mr Bandoza. Pleased to have met you.

Dialogue Build-up

1 John Harrington
2 this is John Harrington
3 Juan, this is John Harrington.

4 Pleased to meet you
5 Pleased to meet you, Mr. er ...

6 Mendoza
7 Juan Mendoza

8 agriculture
9 department of agriculture
10 I'm in the department
11 I'm in the Department of Agriculture

12 What are you studying?

13 Oh, I'm not

14 Pro'fessor Harrington (give also)
14a Professor 'Harrington
15 I'm Pro'fessor Harrington
15a I'm Professor 'Harrington
16 I'm, well, Professor Harrington

17 engineering
18 Professor of Engineering.

19 first year
20 are you in your first year?
21 are you in your first year, Mr er ...?

22 yes and no

23 research student
24 I'm a research student
25 you see, I'm a research student

26 I've arrived
27 I've just arrived
28 I've just arrived here

29 engineering
30 agricultural engineering
31 do something
32 do something in agricultural engineering
33 he's expecting to
34 he's expecting to do something
35 he's expecting to do something in agriculture

36 he's expecting to do something in agricultural engineering.

37 isn't that right?

38 well, well

39 something in common

40 we seem to have something

41 we seem to have something in common

42 we seem to have something in common, Mr Bandoza

43 pleased to have met you

4.2 *Suggested Materials for Episode (ii)*

SITUATION (A)

It is Juan's first morning in the Department: the Secretary is showing him round:

SECRETARY

Now, here's the common room. You are free to come in here anytime and use the facilities.

And through here there's a small reading room.

Room 47. That's the one we use for our main lectures, at any rate. But there are two seminar rooms as well.

Certainly. Just follow me, will you?

JUAN

I see. Fine.

Good. And where will the lectures be?

Do you think you could show me which ones they are, please?

Dialogue Build-up

1 here's the common room
2 now, here's the common room

3 come in here
4 free to come in here
5 you are free to come in here
6 you are free to come in here anytime

7 use the facilities
8 you are free to come in here anytime and use the facilities

9 I see
10 fine
11 through here

12 through here there's a reading room
13 and through here there's a
   small reading room

14 good

15 and where will the lectures
   be?

16 room 47

17 main lectures
18 our main lectures
19 that's the one we use
20 that's the one we use for our
   main lectures
21 at any rate
22 that's the one we use for our
   main lectures, at any rate

23 two seminar rooms
24 there are two seminar rooms
25 but there are two seminar
   rooms as well

26 could you show me
27 do you think you could show
   me
28 which ones they are
29 do you think you could show
   me which ones they are,
   please?

30 certainly

31 just follow me
32 just follow me, will you?

4.3 *Suggested Materials for Episode (iii)*

SITUATION (A)

Shabir is looking for digs: a landlady is showing him round her
house:

LANDLADY

Now here's the lounge. You can
come in here anytime and make
yourself at home.

And through here's the dining
room.

At the end of the landing, on the
left. That's the one we advertised, at any rate. But we've got
two other rooms vacant at the
moment.

On the top floor. Would you like
to have a look at them?

SHABIR

Very kind of you.

Good. And which would be my
room?

Which would those be?

Dialogue Build-up

1 now here's the lounge

2 come in here anytime

3 you can come in here anytime

4 make yourself at home

5 you can come in here anytime and make yourself at home

6 very kind of you

7 the dining room

8 and through here is the dining room

9 good

10 my room

11 and which would be my room?

12 at the end

13 at the end of the landing

14 on the left

15 at the end of the landing on the left

16 the one we advertised

17 that's the one we advertised

18 that's the one we advertised, at any rate

19 we've got two rooms

20 we've got two rooms vacant

21 we've got two other rooms vacant

22 we've got two other rooms vacant at the moment

23 which would those be?

24 on the top floor

25 have a look at them

26 would you like to have a look at them?

SITUATION (B)

Ben is showing Juan round the University:

BEN

See that building over there? That's the Claremont Tower.

Some of the Arts Departments are in there.

Oh yes, that's where the language lab. is.

JUAN

What is it, exactly?

We won't get any lectures in there, I suppose?

Dialogue Build-up

1 see that building

2 see that building over there?

3 Claremont Tower

4 that's the Claremont Tower

5 What is it

6 What is it exactly?

7 Arts Departments

8 some of the Arts Departments

9   some of the Arts Depart-
     ments are in there
10 we won't get any lectures
11 we won't get any lectures in
     there
12 we won't get any lectures in
     there, I suppose?

13 the language lab.
14 that's where the language
     lab. is
15 Oh yes, that's where the lan-
     guage lab. is

Dialogue Application
Using photographs of locations around the University, help pairs of students to build up dialogues identifying different buildings by name, and by the departments and other offices they contain. Each building could be given to a different pair – however, the remainder of the class should be encouraged to contribute, suggest improvements or offer factual corrections.

4.4 *Suggested Materials for Episode (iv)*

SITUATION (A)

MAN 1
Excuse me. Can you tell me where Osborne Road is?

Yes.

I see.

Thanks a lot. Is it far?

MAN 2

Yes. You see that turning down there?

You go down there, that's Jesmond Road, until you come to the second traffic lights.

Then you turn – oh sorry, it's the first set of lights. Turn left, and that's Osborne Road.

Quite a way. Why don't you take a bus? Number 30. It'll be a lot quicker.

Dialogue Build-up
1   excuse me

2   can you tell me
3   Osborne Road

4   can you tell me where
     Osborne Road is?

5   yes (N.B. falling tone)

6 that turning
7 you see that turning
8 you see that turning down there?

9 yes (N.B. rising tone)

10 you go down there
11 the second traffic lights
12 until you come to the second traffic lights
13 you go down there until you come to the second traffic lights
14 that's Jesmond Road
15 you go down there, that's Jesmond Road, until you come to the second traffic lights

16 I see (N.B. rising tone)

17 then you turn
18 the first set of lights

19 oh sorry
20 oh sorry, it's the first set of lights
21 then you turn – oh sorry, it's the first set of lights

22 turn left
23 that's Osborne Road
24 turn left, and that's Osborne Road

25 thanks a lot

26 is it very far?

27 quite a way

28 take a bus
29 why don't you take a bus?

30 number 30

31 a lot quicker
32 it'll be a lot quicker

SITUATION (B)

How would you get to this address? 'Chaddeugh Motors (Spares) Ltd., 43–5 Rye Hill, Newcastle-upon-Tyne.' You are going to ask a friend who knows Newcastle better than you do:

YOU	FRIEND
How do I get to Rye Hill?	
	Your best bet would be down through Grainger Street, I should think. Then through Marlborough Crescent, which is just past Central Station.
You're sure about that?	
	You can check it on a street map if you want.
Is there any other way of getting there? I mean, supposing I walk?	

There's a short cut somewhere behind Newgate. You could ask someone to direct you.

Mmm. Doesn't sound all that easy to me.

Well, those are the only ways I can think of. Unless you can be bothered to go right up Westgate Road or something.

Dialogue Build-up

1 Rye Hill
2 how do I get to Rye Hill?

3 Grainger Street
4 down through Grainger Street
5 I should think
6 down through Grainger Street, I should think
7 your best bet
8 your best bet would be Grainger Street
9 your best bet would be down through Grainger Street
10 your best bet would be down through Grainger Street, I should think

11 Marlborough Crescent
12 then through Marlborough Crescent
13 Central Station
14 just past Central Station
15 then through Marlborough Crescent, which is just past Central Station

16 you're sure about that?

17 check it
18 check it on a street map
19 you can check it on a street map

20 you can check it on a street map if you want

21 is there any way
22 is there any other way
23 is there any other way of getting there?

24 supposing I walk?
25 I mean, suppose I walk?

26 Newgate
27 behind Newgate
28 a short cut behind Newgate
29 there's a short cut behind Newgate
30 there's a short cut somewhere behind Newgate

31 ask someone
32 ask someone to direct you
33 you could ask someone
34 you could ask someone to direct you

35 doesn't sound easy
36 doesn't sound easy to me
37 doesn't sound all that easy to me

38 those are the ways
39 those are the only ways
40 those are the only ways I can think of

41 well, those are the only ways I can think of

42 Westgate Road
43 right up Westgate Road
44 you go right up Westgate Road

45 unless you go right up Westgate Road or something
46 unless you can be bothered to go right up Westgate Road or something

Dialogue Application

(i) Using more photographs or sketches of the University precinct and nearby streets, help pairs of students to build up dialogues on direction-giving, advisability of different routes (e.g. distance; amount of traffic, people, short-cuts). After adequate practice, end by choosing destinations which are 'out of the picture' e.g. the Markets/Central Station/Tyne Bridge.

(ii) Send students out in pairs, each with a fairly well-known destination: each pair should ask passers-by for directions a couple of times. Tell them not to try and memorise the directions they get (they don't even have to follow them) but to listen to *how* people give them. They are to come back within ten minutes or so and discuss their 'findings' and any difficulties they had in comprehension: build some of the 'findings' into a very brief dialogue.

4.5 *Suggested Materials for Episode (v)*

SITUATION (A)

Juan has gone to register for the beginning of the session. The room is full of students, and they are queuing at several desks. He isn't sure what to do, and asks a porter at the door.

JUAN	PORTER
Excuse me. Can you tell me how I register?	
	Yes. You see that desk over there, sir?
Yes.	
	You take your form and letter of acceptance over there. They'll give you your matriculation card.

I see.

> Then you – oh sorry, you haven't got a form yet. They're on the table behind you. Fill it in first.

Thanks very much. Does it take very long?

> Well, there's quite a queue. Why don't you come back in the afternoon, sir? It'll be a lot easier.

(Followed by dialogue build-up on the familiar pattern.)

SITUATION (B)

How would you get hold of this book? 'Simmons, J. S. *et al.*, *Global Epidemiology*: Philadelphia, 1951.' You are going to ask a lecturer who mentioned it during his lecture.

YOU

Excuse me, but how do I get hold of 'Global Epidemiology?'

LECTURER

> Your best bet is the Main Library, I should think. Look under point six, which is up on the fifth floor.

You're sure about that?

> You can check it in the catalogue, if you like.

Is there any other way I can get a copy? I mean, supposing it's not there?

> There's a small library in the Medical School. You could ask them if they've got it.

It doesn't sound all that likely, does it?

> Well that's all I can think of. Unless you can be bothered to buy a copy, or something.

(Followed by dialogue build-up on the familiar pattern.)

REFERENCES

Cole, L. R., 'The Structured Dialogue . . .' *IRAL*, Vol. 7, No. 2, 1969

Cook, V. J., 'Some Types of Oral Structure Drills', *Language Learning*, Vol. 18, Nos. 3 & 4, 1968.
'The Analogy between First and Second Language Learning', *IRAL*, Vol. 7, No. 3, 1969.

Council for Cultural Cooperation (Council of Europe). 'Systems Development in Adult Language Learning', 1973.

James, C., 'The Applied Linguistics of Structured Dialogues', *Language Learning*, Vol. 20, No. 1, 1970.

Newmark, L. and Reibel, D. A., 'Necessity and Sufficiency in Language Learning', *IRAL*, Vol. 6, No. 2, 1968.

Reibel, D. A., 'Language Learning Analysis', *IRAL*, Vol. 7, No. 4, 1969.

Sager, J. C., 'The Language Laboratory and 'Contextual Teaching Methods', *IRAL*, Vol. 7, No. 3, 1969.

Widdowson, H., (Ph.D. Thesis, University of Edinburgh), 1973.

Wilkins, D. A., 'Grammatical Situational and Notional Syllabuses', (Proceedings of 3rd International Congress of Applied Linguistics, 1972.) Julius Groos Verlag, 1972.

7

A Programme in English for Overseas Postgraduate Soil Scientists at the University of Newcastle

R. MACKAY AND A. J. MOUNTFORD

1 Introduction

This paper is divided into two main parts: the first part makes with some general observations about the criteria for the selection and writing of materials for the teaching of English for Special Purposes; the second part is a description of a programme based on reading comprehension prepared for students of Soil Science at the University of Newcastle.

We might start off by saying that if there is any justification for teaching the English of Science and Technology, it lies in enabling the scientist or technologist to communicate adequately with his colleagues about his specialist field of studies, in speech or in writing. Thus, the raison d'être of a service language teaching department is to develop the communicative competence of students in a specific subject area.

Now, as materials writers and teachers faced with a class who are going to be dependent upon us for developing this communicative adequacy, we are entitled to ask the question: how are the needs of the scientist or technologist reflected in current linguistic knowledge and thinking? By linguistics we are not restricting the term narrowly to any one school of thought but refer to the general body of current language description that linguists have put at our disposal.

Very briefly, we think the answer is that we get very little specific help from current linguistic thinking as producers of materials and as teachers of EST. Generally language teachers teach in the units that are presented to them by linguists as the most convenient tools of language analysis. That is, the linguist analyses language using the sentence as the maximum unit and he proceeds down (or up) in a hierarchically ordered arrangement of items through the group and phrase and word and morpheme and phoneme. He says 'Here are the units into which I have analysed language' and we say, 'These are the units by means of which we will teach the language.' And so, if we look at our materials we tend to find sentence-based materials, using the sentence and all the other units that the linguist has used as tools of description. In other words, we base our data intended to facilitate language *acquisition* on units identified as suitable tools for language *description*.

It is generally agreed that while a specialist does not appear to use individual sentence patterns which do not occur in other fields, he does use vocabulary items that do not occur in other fields. But this information is not sufficient for us to produce language teaching materials as it only results in lengthy word lists claiming, as a whole, to be the characteristic feature of this or that field of activity. Michael Halliday, in a recent paper, has said 'special languages may be characterised by different distributions of grammatical patterns, special meanings of generally occurring patterns, and by discourse features of connected text'.[1]

Happily, Halliday suggests that a characterisation of languages for Special Purposes could profitably be approached by moving away from a strictly sentence-based analysis towards an examination of the context. The identification of such characteristic distribution, special meanings of patterns and discourse features of connected text are essential, but in what form do we as teachers, faced with the problem of preparing relevant class material, require this information? We think that the Huddleston report[2] is not of any great use to the language teacher. He seems to side step the principal question which is 'How is the language of this field of activity different from the language of that field of activity?'

We do not want only percentage counts of how frequently this or that item occurs, and we don't want simply structural descriptions of patterns which occur more frequently than others. We want a description in terms of the communicative value of the language being used by the scientist or technologist at any particular point. For example, we don't merely want to be told that the modal verb '*will*' is more frequent than the '*going to* infinitive' in the language of mechanical engineering. But we do want to know what the communicative or rhetorical value of '*will*' is – when it is being used to express the concept of potentiality as opposed to that of futurity, as in, for example, the following statement:

This motor will produce X horsepower at 3,500 r.p.m.

If the overseas student interprets this as a statement about some future activity and waits for this to happen, he may wait for a very long time. The demonstrator in this case is explaining what the motor is capable of and not predicting a future burst of activity of the motor.

We need to know, on the one hand, the communicative value of the language pattern, as well as, on the other, its structural description and likelihood of occurrence in a particular field. A description of its structure could help to give us grammatical correctness, a statement of its communicative or rhetorical value would help to give us communicative adequacy or appropriateness in a given context and co-text. These aspects are essentially complementary in accounting for the whole 'language event'. And this language event need not be restricted to one sentence in length.

We use the words 'language event' a Firthian term – because it describes a useful concept. It also points to the fact that we will get more stimulus from the 'London School of Linguistics' than we will get from the transformational generative school – a more strictly codified approach, interested in language data insofar as it can be accounted for by a generative mechanism. To do this, the linguist must start abstracting and once this happens he is forced to ignore elements vital to the communicative process. Thus, that transformational generative grammar is of minimal importance to us so far and that an approach which admits and includes all channels of communication in its final description is of maximal importance to us.

So we need organisational framework for our language data, not in terms solely of traditional linguistic units or even sentence structures, but linguistic forms of a communicative kind – procedures, concepts, events indispensable to the scientist or technologist and which manifest themselves in varieties of structures.

Scientific language data – the kind of data we would be drawing upon as teachers of English to scientists – particularly lends itself to examination in such terms since the scientist is constantly involved in performing fairly explicit acts of defining, identifying, comparing, differentiating, classifying, etc. These are basic procedural acts relating to the methodology of science. We are not suggesting that the scientist is the only one who performs these acts – we all perform them in everyday life – but the scientist appears to make such procedures explicit in various ways in his use of language.

We can show this schematically.

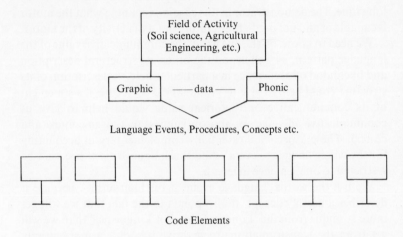

We can start with field of Activity. The language needs of the student are not met by presenting the accumulated knowledge of the entire field to him. We select data from that field, and we select that data, depending upon the language skills we wish to teach, from written texts (for reading skills) or from spoken lectures (for aural skills) – both skills of importance to postgraduates.

Whatever the medium and areas within it selected as data, the scientist is involved in putting over certain concepts, in talking about certain procedures which reflect activity in the laboratory, workshop, etc.

So we have a set of procedures and concepts or 'language events' and these are made up of code elements – the words, the structures, the patterns, the combinations of patterns that have been necessary to express the events.

Applying this schema to the material developed in this paper, the Field of Activity is Soil Science, the data is a set of written texts. This data reflects the procedures which are essential to the soil scientist and which distinguish his organisation of sentence patterns and groups of sentence patterns from that of the salesman or the waiter.

The next step, then, once the communicative function of the language event has been identified is to describe the code elements of these procedures. These procedures may be realised in the code elements of the language in several different ways. We are going to get a set of alternatives for any particular concept or procedure – for example there are many ways of expressing purpose in the written medium:

1 The $\left\{\begin{array}{l}\text{purpose}\\\text{aim}\\\text{object}\end{array}\right\}$ of the safety valve is to permit excess pressure to escape.

2 A safety valve is provided $\left\{\begin{array}{l}\text{to}\\\text{so as to}\\\text{in order to}\\\text{for the purpose of}\\\text{with the object of}\\\text{with the aim of}\\\text{with a view to}\end{array}\right\}\left\{\begin{array}{l}\text{allow etc.}\\\text{allowing etc.}\end{array}\right.$

3 A safety valve is provided $\left\{\begin{array}{l}\text{so that}\\\text{in order that}\end{array}\right\}$ the steam may, etc.

We do not think for the purposes of teaching reading at the level of our students in Newcastle that we are entitled to restrict that set to only one or two alternatives.

2 The Situation

The admission requirements for postgraduate studies in the University of Newcastle upon Tyne include the taking of an obligatory language proficiency test administered by the Language Centre. Intending students are obliged to take the test before registering, not necessarily to score a 'pass'. Students scoring below a 'cut-off point' are recommended to attend remedial English Language classes in the Language Centre. This system, while ensuring that the best foreign specialists are not excluded on language grounds, carries with it the problem that students are admitted whose mastery of English is markedly inadequate to permit them to fulfil the requirements of the department in which they wish to study or research.

In 1970 a lecturer was appointed to take responsibility for catering for the language needs of non-native English speaking students of which class there are currently between 450 and 500 in the University.

This task involved four principal steps:

(i) identifying those students whose academic success appears to be seriously threatened by inadequate English;

(ii) determining the language needs of these students as dictated by the particular demands made upon them by the nature of their academic and practical work;

(iii) preparing appropriate teaching/learning materials to meet these needs adequately;

(iv) conducting the practical teaching tasks involved in preparing these students linguistically to take their place alongside their native English speaking fellows.

Step (i) could be most economically dealt with by the introduction of a compulsory diagnostic test, administered during the first weeks of term, for all overseas students for whom English is not their mother tongue. However, due to opposition to this plan the lecturer in charge of remedial English had to rely on problem students being referred to him by tutors and professors. Native English-speaking specialists in the sciences, applied sciences and agriculture frequently tend to under-estimate quantity and quality of language use required by the overseas student to ensure success in his course. (Likewise they tend to underestimate the time and effort the overseas student must expend in order to achieve the necessary minimum.) Moreover, since a tutor's assessment of an overseas student's English is usually the result of a face to face interview, initially, only those students with a marked lack of fluency or serious inability to comprehend in an informal interview situation are referred. Less easily identifiable language weaknesses closely related to the requirements of the course such as understanding lectures, taking adequate notes, the ability to read speedily and accurately and the skill to write answers to examination questions, progress reports and dissertations all on specialised topics, tend to be initially overlooked. Such weaknesses may only come to light late in the course when there is insufficient time for them to be remedied. Thus, the Language Centre attempts to keep in as close personal contact as possible with the specialist departments and interviews and tests overseas students as early in the academic year as possible. A full list of all overseas students registered in the University is available from the computer in the second half of November.

Once students in need of special English instruction are identified, the administrative problem of grouping them together in classes according to some pedagogically convenient criterion has to be met. This criterion could be the present level of attainment in English, mother tongue or field of specialised study. However, since almost all English tuition must be fitted into 'free' hours in a variety of heavily loaded departmental timetables this method of grouping is not always possible.

Thus, any truly effective language programme must have the following characteristics:

(i) it must be capable of being used with students from a wide variety of language backgrounds in the same class;

(ii) it must be capable of being used in classes of students of mixed attainment in English.

None of these students, however, would be complete beginners in the language. Since they come from a number of countries whose English Language teaching standards vary widely, they do not fall into an adequately labelled category such as 'intermediate' or 'advanced'. Nevertheless, all would have studied English as a 'subject' at School or University during the previous ten or twelve years; none would have used English as a medium of Education.

(iii) it must be capable of being used with students who have varying amounts of time to spend studying English;

and (iv) it must, as far as possible, be self instructional or at least be capable of being used by students with only a limited amount of contact hours with the English instructor.

This last point (iv) is, in our opinion, of great importance not only because it influences the structure and writing of the programmes but because it acknowledges the immeasurable importance of the student's own efforts to master the language. It explicitly acknowledges the difference between 'teaching' and 'learning'.

'Teaching' involves the selection and organisation of the language data considered necessary or appropriate for the task and the presentation of it in the most suitable way in the workbook, classroom or language laboratory. When a class of students is fairly homogeneous as regards mother tongue, attainment, time dedicated to the programme and general ability, the materials writer has a strong basis on which to include or exclude this or that item or piece of language data. However, when the materials writer is faced with such a variety of variables as in Newcastle upon Tyne the onus must necessarily fall more heavily upon the individual student. We have no sound criterion for deciding that, for example, the student of soil science must learn to *produce* the form:

> Bacterial symbiosis is the relationship of mutual benefit between bacteria and plants.

as a way of defining the process of bacterial symbiosis, but that he needs only to *recognise* such stylistic variations as:

> The relationship of mutual benefit between bacteria and plants is known as bacterial symbiosis.
> The relationship of mutual benefit between bacteria and plants is called bacterial symbiosis.
> Bacterial symbiosis may be defined as the relationship of mutual benefit between bacteria and plants.
> The relationship of mutual benefit between bacteria and plants is termed bacterial symbiosis.
> The meaning of bacterial symbiosis is the relationship of mutual benefit between bacteria and plants.

Such restriction applied throughout the language data would certainly lighten the learning load on the student but we feel that such a practice would be unjustified in this situation given our present state of knowledge of varieties and registers. Current research being done by R. Straker Cook, University of Edinburgh on the 'verbal routines' from which a selection may be made to suit specifiable conditions within any specified field may throw more light on this important area and serve to give us objective information upon which to base such restrictions in the future.

Thus we have chosen to offer all the common stylistic variations the student might encounter in, in this instance, specialised textbooks and let him choose any one, or more than one structure for the purpose of production in his own writing. These stylistic variations are the result of the rapid reading of a number of textbooks which the student would be required to be familiar with.

This procedure could be and has been criticised from the point of view of the teacher of a homogeneous group where he believes that his task is not only to expose his students to well-arranged ways of communicating certain types of information but also 'to select and guide his students through that small sub-set of the possible ways that he feels are both most useful to them and appropriate to their level of competence in the language'.*

We would, for the present, defend it on the grounds that

(i) any choice of one productive pattern would, at present, be arbitrarily based;

(ii) placing such a restriction on the choice of 'productive patterns' tends to lead to puzzlement in the student. He tends, no matter what may be said about the status of the 'recognition patterns' presented, to regard them as somehow 'inferior' to the 'productive pattern'.

(iii) At the level at which our students are operating – both in English and in their specialist field – we have no control whatsoever over their language intake outside the English class. They will read and hear a great variety of patterns appropriate to one situation. We feel that part of our task is to expose them to the variety of appropriate patterns so that their recognition difficulties may be minimised and that their productive repertoire may be as rich as they have the time and motivation to allow.

3 The Specific Needs

The professional performance of the overseas specialist studying or researching in a British University must necessarily compare favourably with that of their native English speaking fellow students. In other words, they must learn to master the skills requisite for taking in information of a specialist nature by

(a) listening to and understanding lectures and discussions probably summarising important information in note form:
(b) reading journals and textbooks in their own field fluently and efficiently.

They must also master the skills to communicate their new learning or research findings.

(c) taking an active oral part in tutorial classes and other discussion groups;

* John Swales, University of Leeds: personal communication.

d) preparing papers and reports, answers to examination questions, and in the case of M.Sc. and Ph.D. students, producing a full length dissertation using the characteristics of 'specialised' continuous discourse.

4 Developing Reading Skill

A great deal of time has to be spent by post-graduate students reading texts selected by their tutors and lecturers. It was the purpose of this part of the programme* to develop the student's performance in comprehending written English. We wanted to design materials that would enable the student to interpret texts with greater accuracy. Such materials should provoke controlled linguistic responses, and provide for the student insights into the syntactic structure of English as exemplified by the language of Soil Science. It was felt that to be relevant our texts should be closely modelled on the language students would be likely to find on opening a text book on Soil Science. They needed to be taught, therefore, techniques of reading comprehension that would enable them to understand 'authentic' texts without the aid of a teacher. In other words, they had to be taught a strategy of reading. Such a strategy should enable them to scan any text in order to ascertain its broad content and, on closer study, extract essential information.

In this connection, it should be remembered that although reading comprehension is often called a receptive skill, as opposed to the productive skill of writing, it is a mistake to regard it as passive. It would perhaps be more accurate, as C. V. James has noted, to regard reading skills as *perceptive*, 'representing not passive states but exceedingly active processes'.[3] In order to read efficiently, a student has to perceive and interpret not only lexical meaning but grammatical and rhetorical structure. The activity of interpretation requires the simultaneous perception and understanding of not only word meanings but relationships between words, within and between sentences, within and between paragraphs. An understanding of how texts are organised is an essential part of what we mean by developing a reading strategy. While devising the programme the following questions were borne in mind.

* Part II of the unified syllabus described in Chapter 6.

1 *Grammar:* What structural patterns of English could be identified in a selection of texts drawn from textbooks on Soil Science? Our analysis – conducted in informal and traditional terms – concentrated on the structure of the verb phrase, the structure of the noun phrase, and sentence embedding and conjunction.

2 *Lexis:* What lexical items and collocations appeared to characteristically belong to the field of discourse of Soil Science? Again, an informal list was drawn up which was in no sense exhaustive, but a useful adhoc pedagogic inventory based on our texts.

3 *Cohesion:* What devices of cohesion in our texts appeared to be important? By devices of cohesion we mean, in particular, pronominal cohesion of various kinds, and what might be called rhetorical cohesion – the use of certain inter-sentential connectives to mark the relationship of one part of the discourse to another. For example, the relationship of contrast marked by *however, on the other hand*; the relationship of addition marked by *moreover*; and of consequence marked by *consequently, therefore* etc.

5 Selection and Grading of Texts

5.1 *Selection of Texts*

Eleven texts were chosen and distributed over five units of work, each unit representing two weeks work. The texts were chosen and arranged in such a way as to form as far as possible within a ten week course an introduction in English to the subject of Soil Science. Clearly, the subject was in no way delimited by our choice of texts. However, certain fundamental aspects were selected and put in a logical order. A certain amount of simplification was performed on texts to make them pedagogically presentable. This involved loosening the texture of the language to isolate and emphasise a point of linguistic interest, or to render the content of the text more easily interpretable. Complex nominal groups were sometimes expanded into sentences, and complex sentences were sometimes divided up, introducing an anaphoric expression to which the students' attention could be drawn in the exercises.

The texts themselves ranged from an elementary introduction to the origin of soil, through classifications of soil, descriptions and analyses of particular soil types, to a discussion of the physical, chemical and biological properties of soil. It was assumed all the time that the language teacher was not teaching Soil Scientists Soil Science. However, the course aimed at exploiting the soil scientist's knowledge of his subject to illustrate the kind of linguistic communication characteristic of the subject. The language teacher, therefore, was expected to master the subject content and the language content of the texts.

5.2 *Grading of Texts*

5.2.1 LINGUISTIC

The texts were graded according to the following criteria:

(a) Length of text: the texts of the first two units were single paragraph texts, whereas those of units four and five were of two or three paragraphs. Thus, comprehension had to be sustained over a longer stretch of discourse in later units. Devices of cohesion were inter-paragraph in later units as well as inter-sentential.

(b) Sentences were descriptively more complex in later units than in earlier ones. Using the traditional terms simple, compound and complex, the texts of Unit 10 contained 10 simple sentences with expanded noun phrases, 2 complex sentences with subordinate clauses and 1 compound sentence. Text 1 of Unit 5 contained 2 simple sentences with expanded noun phrase, 1 compound sentence, 10 complex sentences and 2 sentences in which there were subordinating clauses.

(c) There was also an increase in the complexity of the noun phrase. The texts of later units contained noun phrases which employed descriptively more complex nominal compounds than those of earlier units. In addition, there were noun phrases containing more deleted structural items and with more anaphoric reference. Thus the later units are pedagogically more difficult as well as descriptively more complex.

5.2.2 RHETORICAL

The scientist has 'systematic and highly sophisticated methods for managing and understanding happenings. A useful way of studying the methods of the sciences is to imagine them as means for answering certain kinds of questions about happenings'.[4] Thus, the scientist asks such questions about objects, processes and operations as 'What is it?' or 'What are its properties or its functions?' He also asks of events 'What happened?', 'How did it happen?' He formulates hypotheses and conducts experiments to verify such hypotheses which may later be elevated to rules and laws.

The questions that the scientist asks, and the answers that follow, are reflected in the kind of linguistic communication that the scientist employs. The scientist defines, classifies, generalises, describes, predicts and observes events etc. These acts of communication are paralleled by the expository techniques of definition, classification, generalisation, description, prediction and observation etc. We may also refer to such techniques as rhetorical acts.[5] These rhetorical acts can be used to organise the language of scientific and technical English in the preparation of teaching materials. They can be observed in any scientific study – Chemistry, Physics, the Earth Sciences, and in the Sciences of Human Behaviour, Psychology, Economics etc. – though with perhaps different degrees of emphasis. For example, classification is probably more widespread in the Biological Sciences than, say, in Physics.

Thus, texts may be selected and graded according to the rhetorical function they perform. Such an approach has the virtue of taking into account the communicative purposes for which language is used by scientists. It also provides a framework for the composition of exercises that relate different linguistic structures to a common communicative act.

For our purpose in constructing a syllabus for Soil Scientists we conflated the expository technique of analysis and description into analytic description of properties, of processes, of states and of operations. Units on hypothesising or prediction were not developed, nor were units on inductive and deductive reasoning, although the associated linguistic features are of considerable importance.*

The texts were grouped and ordered in the following way.

Title of Text	Units	Rhetorical Act
1 The origin of soil	1	Formal definition
2 Rocks and their deserved soils 3 Textural classification of soils 4 Soil groups	2	Classification

---

* Such rhetorical acts have been developed into units of teaching material in the *English in Focus* series published by OUP. See Chapter 3.

Title of Text	*Units*	*Rhetorical Act*
5 The physical properties of soil 6 Podzols 7 Latosols	3	Informal definition Description of properties Description of processes
8 Soil Layers 9 The chemical composition of soil	4	Description of states Description of properties
10 The function of soil micro-organism	5	Description of properties Description of processes Classification
11 Microbiological analysis of soil		Description of operation

It should be noted that some of the texts combine different rhetorical acts; for example, Text 5 in Unit 3, and Text 10 in Unit 5. Any piece of written discourse draws on many and various rhetorical forms to achieve its purpose. What we did was to isolate a particular feature of the discourse and make it the focus of the unit. This pedagogic technique applies also to the lexical and grammatical patterns studied in each unit. They are not only to be found in the unit in which they are studied in detail.

6 The Grammar Syllabus

6.1 *Selection and Grading of Structures*

As the course was designed primarily as a reading comprehension course, it was only logical that the grammar part of the syllabus should be derived from the accompanying texts. Such a text-based syllabus has certain advantages in that exercises on grammatical structure can be clearly related to a corpus of language. However, there is always the danger of omitting from the course particular structural forms that individual students may have difficulty in manipulating in any productive work. This is an inherent problem in remedial teaching and cannot simply be solved by basing structural work on error analysis. What is required is a design which relates structural work back to reading comprehension, that anticipates reading difficulties at the structural level. Thus, the grammar exercises aim at focussing attention on the meaning of grammatical forms, and particular emphasis placed on ways of expressing a particular meaning employing a variety of surface structures. Here again the notional basis of the syllabus was an advantage

For example, the concepts of cause – reason – result are semantically related. However, they can be expressed in a variety of ways in English. By using a 'spiral' technique in setting out the grammatical patterns of the syllabus it is possible to examine the various syntactic means available to express cause – reason – result at various times in the course, and relate them to each other. Unit 1 contained exercises on connectors of logical sequence between sentences such as *thus, therefore, so, consequently, as a result* etc. There were also exercises on various nominal expressions of cause – reason – result, e.g. *B is a/the result of A*; *the cause of B is A*; *the reason for B is A*; *the consequence of A is B*; *the effect of A is B*. Later in Unit 3 in dealing with the expository technique, the description of a process, the rhetorical pattern restriction/condition/circumstance – process – statement of result/effect was examined. Finally in Unit 4 various intra-sentential subordinate clauses of purpose, result (or non-result) and reason were exercised. Comparison and relative clause modification were similarly introduced, reinforced later, or re-introduced in different transformational guises. Each new aspect of a semantic or conceptual system was built upon a previous syntactic pattern, which was thus given a wider reference. The teacher not only dealt with a pattern as illustrated in a particular text, but also was required to refer back to previous texts where the item or structure was also used but not focussed on in that unit. In other words, he would travel back down the spiral as well as move up round it. It was assumed that most of the points contained in the syllabus had been previously taught at some time in the students' linguistic history. The point we were concerned with was applying an existing 'knowledge' of particular grammatical forms to the English of Soil Science, and showing new ways of expressing familiar concepts, or relating different surface forms to a common semantic framework.

6.2 *Unit Design*

Each unit was divided into two broad areas of interest:

(a) inter-sentential relationships in the structure of the text; and

(b) intra-sentential relationships. In the former the expository technique and the means to achieve it were considered. In addition, this part of the syllabus was concerned with the way connectives are used to achieve cohesion between sentences within a paragraph. These were ordered in the following way.

Unit 1: *Resultative*
    e.g. thus, therefore, as a result, so,
    Enumerative (dynamic sequence)
    e.g. at first, initially,
        Then, later on, subsequently,
        finally, eventually,
Unit 2: *Illustrative*
    e.g. for example, for instance, such as,
        which include/consist of,
Unit 3: *Explicative*
    e.g. that is, in other words, meaning,
        namely, which is called, in short
        A, or B, (A = B)
Unit 4: *Contrastive*
e.g. however, nevertheless, yet, on the other hand,
    Enumerative (static sequence)
    e.g. first(ly), second(ly),
        third(ly),
Unit 5: *Additive*
    e.g. moreover, further-more, in addition, similarly,
    Summative
    e.g. thus, therefore, in conclusion.

At the intra-sentential level, we were concerned with (i) the sentence as a unit in a stream of discourse and the deployment of clause adjuncts, in particular relative clauses; (ii) the structure of the verb phrase within the sentence – tense, aspect, voice and modality – and verb formation; and (iii) the structure of the noun phrase where the focus of interest was levelled at the formation of nominals, adjectival phrases, affixation and nominal compounds. Although our focus in this part of the syllabus was on the noun phrase, the exercises necessarily related the noun phrase to the structure of the sentence.

    The topics covered in the syllabus can be shown as follows.

A: *The structure of the text:*
  1 Expository technique
  2 Cohesion: inter-sentential connectives

B: *The structure of the sentence:*
  1 Relative clause modification
  2 Comparison
    Causation
    Condition
    Degree
    Concession
    Purpose
  3 Expressing concurrency of events
    Expressing alternatives

C: *The structure of the verb phrase:*
  1 'Be'
    'Resemble'
  2 Voice
    Tense
    Aspect
  3 Modality
  4 Verb formation

D: *The structure of the noun phrase:*
  Nominalisation
  Nominal compounds
  Adjectivalisation
  Affixation

6.3 *Outline of Unit 1*

The following is the outline for Unit 1.

  A: *The structure of the text*
  1 *Expository technique*
    Formal definition:
    (a) A is B = B is known as A
              B is termed A
              B is called A
    (b) A is B which C = B which C is known as A
                                  is called A
    (c) A means B
           A may be defined as B

2 *Cohesion: inter-sentential connectives*
  Resultative:
    Thus, therefore, as a result, so.
  Enumerative:
    at first, initially,
    then, later on, subsequently,
    finally, eventually,

B: *The Structure of the sentence*
1 *Comparison*
  (a) syntactic: less/more ... than
                 adj – er ... than
                 less/more + adj ... than
                 ADJ – est, least, most.
  (b) semantic: making explicit comparative forms
                which are implied by the conjunction
                of lexical items.

2 *Causation*
  → A causes B
  → B is the result of A
  → cause of B is A
  → reason for B is A
  → consequence of A is B
  → A results in B
  → the effect of AA is B

C: *The structure of the verb phrase*
1 *BE*
  (a) NP + BE + Prep. Phrase (Existential locative)
      → THERE + BE + NP + Prep. phrase
      → NP + HAVE + NP + Prep. phrase
  (b) NP + BE + Adj (Characterising)
  (c) NP_1 + BE + NP_2 (Classifying)

2 *RESEMBLE*
  Be like = look like = similar to = resemble.

D: *The structure of the noun phrase*
1 *Nominal compounds*
  $N_1 + N_2$ + BE + Adj → Adj + $N_2 + N_1$
  e.g. residues of minerals are insoluble → insoluble mineral
  residues

2   *Nominalisation*
   (a) V – N ion (i.e. the result of V is N ion e.g. erode –
       erosion)
   (b) Be like = similarity/resemblance between
       have similarity/resemblance to.

7 Reading Comprehension Questions and Exercises

When designing class exercises we made a distinction between
comprehension questions and comprehension exercises. The former
were designed to elicit from the student information about the
content of the text; in other words, to test his understanding of
the text. The comprehension exercises were designed to enable the
student to understand how the text functioned as a linguistic entity.
Such exercises clearly related to our aim of developing for the student
a strategy of reading.

   The design of the comprehension questions needs little comment.
They included *true/false statements* about the text, *yes/no questions*
about certain stated or implied facts, and *wh-questions*. It should be
remembered that a student does not develop a skill merely by
answering questions on a text. However, such questions are a
standard pedagogic procedure and have some value in rehearsing
what the student has understood about the content of the text. *Wh-
questions*, it should be noted, require language production, and
consequently it can be difficult at times to know whether a wrong
answer is due to miscomprehension, or an inadequate productive
facility. However, comprehension questions do not usually focus in
any precise way on how the student understands the text if they are
restricted simply to the content of the text. Thus, different kinds of
questions were designed, the purpose of which was to exercise the
students' comprehension skill rather than test it.

   The first set focussed on vocabulary. It was clear that students
needed to be taught certain features of the vocabulary of their subject
specialisation, as evidenced by the texts. They needed to recognise (a)
when words and phrases are more formal equivalents to words and
phrases of the 'common-core' of English e.g., from the text quoted
below, *residue, derived from, composed of*; (b) when certain
expressions from the 'common-core' of English are used with a
particular meaning different from the more general use, e.g. *parent*
rock, weathering *agent*; and (c) those words which are unique to
particular subject specialisations and which rarely occur outside it,

e.g. *leaching, deflocculation, salinisation.* Of course, there are other features of lexis the understanding of which requires exercising; in particular, nominalisation, affixations and compound nouns. However, these were dealt with, as can be seen from the outline syllabus above, in the grammar section of each unit.

There are various ways of exercising vocabulary. The way we chose was one which required the student to match an expression from the text to a paraphrase, as follows: Instead of saying/talking about A (the paraphrase in the context in which it occurs in the text) ... the writer says/talks about/uses the expression B (expression from the text) ... We judged this better than disembodied expressions for which equivalents have to be found from the text because of the appearance of both the paraphrase and the expression sought in one complete sentence. It should be remembered, however, that offering paraphrases of technical terms does not imply that they are equivalent in any communicative sense. The expression *made up of* although in certain circumstances a paraphrase of the word *composed* is not equivalent in textual or communicative value to the word *composed.* Herein lies the danger of offering such paraphrases, of explaining vocabulary: a kind of register mixing. More purely technical terms such as *leaching* or *deflocculation* are, however, definable in a rigorous way. We attempted to provide exercises in such formal definition making, as defining is one of the rhetorical acts we were focussing on. It has not only a metalingual function, and thereby a pedagogic function, but also a communicative function in the subject itself for advanced students of Soil Science. Certain expressions were paraphrased or defined *within* the text (remembering that our texts were not simply lifted from textbooks, but prepared for teaching purposes). There are certain linguistic devices commonly used by writers to do this, and the function of our exercises was to draw students attention to such devices. The devices we had in mind included A, or B ... (where A and B are two different words which refer to the same thing), and explicative phrase such as *that is to say, by which we mean, in other words* etc.

The other linguistic aspect of the texts our comprehension exercises focussed on was that of cohesion. We were interested in getting the student to understand how texts cohere grammatically, and how they cohere rhetorically. Grammatical cohesion is achieved through anaphoric devices of pronominalisation and substitution/repetition.[6] This can be easily handled by exercises that get the student to identify what particular anaphoric expressions refer back to in the text, or by offering grammatically possible referents in a multiple choice format. This, of course, is a simple enough exercise and students are unlikely to get any of the exercises wrong – though it was surprising how often careless reading led to an incorrect identification that inevitably would have led to faulty comprehension.* The point of the exercise lies not in its difficulty or otherwise but in it being a comprehension procedure that a student should be trained to do while reading.

There are two aspects of rhetorical cohesion: the intra-sentential, in which sentences stand in a particular relationship to one another indicated by subordinating conjunctions such as *because, although, whenever* etc.; and inter-sentential, in which the relationships between sentences are marked by connectives such as *however, moreover, for example* etc. We were particularly interested in this latter kind of cohesion because it has to do with the communicative value that particular sentences have in discourse – a generalisation followed by an illustration, or observations followed by a deduced generalisation, or contrasting assertions etc. This was exercised in a number of ways. Students were given a rhetorical framework into which sentences, or groups of sentences, had to be placed to form a coherent whole. Sometimes blanks were left in the text and students were asked to supply the correct connective from a list. On other occasions students were asked to put a jumbled series of sentences in the correct order, which also necessitated attention to the devices of cohesion the sentences contained.

There were two other sets of exercises that were important. The first were labelled *prediction* exercises and the second *transformation* exercises. Two exercise formats for prediction were used. A short text (either part of or derived from the main text) was presented and closed. The student had to predict on the basis of rhetorical semantic and grammatical clues the word that best filled the blank space. Alternatively, the student was asked to complete a sentence, or sentences, from a list of expressions. Transformation exercises required the student to manipulate the syntactic structure of a sentence either to get an underlined expression in subject position, or to bring to the surface a semantic element implicit in the sentence, which sometimes involved changing its rhetorical force. For example, instead of saying *soil is a residue which results from the weathering of rocks and the decomposition of plant and animal materials,* which is a

---

* Expressions like *this,* as in the preceding sentence above, often caused difficulty because they refer to a complete idea that in actual text may have been developed over a whole paragraph.

formal definition, we can say *when rocks are weathered and plant and animal materials decomposed, the residue is soil*, which is an observation.

A common practice in language teaching materials is to present sentence patterns as models for sentence production. Such sentence patterns are presented in isolation, the implication being that there is only one way of expressing the semantic content of the sentence. Little attempt is made to show how much sentence patterns can be transformed by thematising particular elements of the sentence. To give a very simple example, take the sentence *John gave Bill a book*. This sentence can be easily converted into *John gave a book to Bill*. However, from the point of view of its possible occurrence in discourse other variants are just as likely: *A book was given to Bill by John. Bill was given a book by John. It was John who gave the book to Bill* etc. These surface structure variations in sentence patterns are not merely stylistic variants. They occur according to how the writer chooses to sequence the information he is presenting. Thus the ordering of given and new information determines the way in which the discourse develops, and the particular sentence patterns that will be chosen to express this information. Only in an abstracted and contextless sense could it be said that the pattern contained in the sentence *John gave Bill a book* is prior, or more basic, or important, than any of the others. Yet this is often what is implied by teaching such patterns in isolation. It is small wonder that students encounter difficulties in structuring a text while reading. It is not only unfamiliar lexis that causes the problems of interpretation; it is also the unfamiliarity with discourse variants of familiar sentence patterns that causes uncertainty and faltering comprehension. This is as true of definition patterns, and cause and result patterns, as it is of the simple direct/indirect object patterns quoted above. Indeed, the choice between active and passive verb forms is often more dependent on the distribution of information in a text than on any wish for impersonality, or grammatical focussing on the receiver or sufferer of the action. It is often dependent, in scientific writing at least, on the need to express resultant states rather than active processes. Exercises which draw the student's attention to such discourse transformations, reflecting in Halliday's terms the textual function of language, are crucial in building up the student's confidence by equipping him with a strategy of how to structure texts, and, thus, how to interpret them faster and more accurately.

8 Sample Teaching Material

The following is a sample unit for the programme. It should be noted that only two examples of each exercise are included.

Unit 1

TEXT

The origin of soil

Soil is a residue which results from the weathering of rocks and the decomposition of plant and animal materials. The materials other than organic matter are derived under natural conditions from rocks of various kinds. Alternate expansion and contraction causes rocks to split. At first these cracks break huge masses of rock into large boulders. Then these are cracked into smaller boulders. Subsequently different agents break down these rocks into finer and finer particles. The process continues till eventually small stones, gravel and sand form the basis of soil. In the parent rock is its chemical and mineralogical composition. In humid regions, in addition to physical processes of weathering or erosion, rock particles are affected by the solvent action of water. The water may contain carbonic acid and other strong acids. Consequently, great changes in the physical and chemical composition of the soil takes place. The insoluble mineral residues have little resemblance to the original rocks, and a large part of the soil contains amounts of organic residues.

COMPREHENSION QUESTIONS

1 Vocabulary

One characteristic of this passage is that the writer is using certain formal scientific terms to express his ideas.

i Instead of saying that soil is made up of rock particles he says that soil is .... of rock particles.

ii Instead of saying that soil is something that is left behind or remains over he says soil is a ....

Complete these sentences by putting the words below into the spaces provided.

a Soil is a .... which results from the .... of rocks, and the .... of .... matter.

   organic, decomposition, weathering, residue

b .... and .... causes rock to split.

   contraction, alternate, expansion.

2 *True or false?*

Write TRUE or FALSE after these statements:
a The result of weathering is the formation of soil. ....
b Organic matter is derived from rocks of various kinds ....

3 *Implications*

In the last exercise we were concerned with what the writer actually SAID or STATED. In this exercise we shall be concerned with what he IMPLIED. To imply means to mean something but not actually state it. For example:

Does the writer imply that the soil contains other matter than that which comes from rock?

Answer: Yes, he does.

REASON: Because he says soil is a residue from the weathering of rocks AND the decomposition of organic matter.

Now you do these. Think of reasons for your answers.
a Does the writer imply that the heat of the sun is an erosion agent?
b Does the writer imply that physical processes of erosion are more important in humid regions than in arid regions?

4 *Answer these questions*

You may answer either YES or NO. Try and give reasons for your answers.
a Is organic matter derived from weathering? ....
b Are boulders larger than stones and gravel? ....

5 *Anaphora*

a In line 2 what does the phrase *organic matter* refer back to? ....
b What does *these cracks* refer to in line 4? ....

6 *Prediction*

Complete these sentences with one of the words or phrases below.
a Soil is formed from the erosion of rocks and the decomposition of
....
  i) natural conditions
  ii) organic matter
  iii) carbonic acid
  iv) chemicals
b If rocks alternately expand and contract day after day eventually they will ....
i) decompose ii) weather iii) crack iv) break down

7 Cohesion
A A short description of the weathering process could be built up like this.
At first, ... Then, ... Subsequently, ...
Eventually ....

Now you insert these sentences into the blank spaces in the correct order.
a This process goes on until small stones, gravel and sand form the basis of soil.
b These are split into smaller boulders.
c Different agents break down these rocks into finer particles.
d Huge masses of rock are broken into large boulders.

B In the blank spaces in the passage below insert the appropriate logical connector from those given:
Erosion procession in arid regions is largely physical, ... the chemical and mineralogical composition of the soil closely resembles the parent rock. .... in regions of high rainfall, rock particles are affected by the solvent action of water, ... the soil is very different from the parent rock because great changes occur in its physical and chemical composition.
Subsequently, consequently, however, so, alternatively, nevertheless, therefore.

8 Transformation (Paraphrase)
A i Instead of saying soil is a residue which results from the weathering of rocks and the decomposition of plant and animal materials, we can say when rocks are weathered and plant and animal materials ...., the .... is ....
ii Instead of saying alternate expansion and contraction causes rocks to split, we can say the splitting of rocks ....

B Complete the sentences below beginning with the phrase given, e.g.
i Soil is a residue which ....
ii The weathering of rocks and ....
That which results as *a residue from the weathering of rocks and* the decomposition of plant and material is called soil.

Unit

A STRUCTURE OF THE TEXT

1 Expository technique
Formal definition

We use a formal definition in scientific discourse in order to state as exactly as possible what a term means. Formal definitions often follow the formula:

Term = class + sum of differences. The language pattern we use to express this is:

A is B which C
or: B which C is known as A
or: B which C is called A

Look at these examples:

a Soil is a residue which results from the weathering of rocks and the decomposition of plant and animal materials.

b Enzymes are substances produced by living cells which can bring about chemical reactions.

Notice: in each case the (*sum of differences*) is introduced by a relative clause introduced by *which* (or '*that*'). When a (*process*) is the class into which the term fits, we use the phrase (*by which*) to introduce the second part of the definition.

Now look at these examples:

a A residue which results from the weathering of rocks and the decomposition of plant and animal materials is known as soil.

b Substances produced by living cells which can bring about chemical reactions are called enzymes.

You write c and d like the above.

i Now, expand these into full definitions:

a Corrosion – process – ground and surface water dissolves and chemically alters rock materials.

b A soil horizon – a layer of soil with distinct characteristics – it is produced by soil forming processes.

ii Complete the gaps in the following definitions with words or phrases from the list below. You must also insert BE and WHICH.

a Aerobics .... play the most beneficial part in agriculture.

b .... the quality of a soil horizon ....

iii Match the terms below to these descriptions.

a A material that increases the rate of a chemical reaction.

b The portion of soil water which is held by cohesion as a continuous film around the particles and in the spaces between the grains of soil.

c Nitrogen-containing organic compounds which link together in the formation of a protein molecule.

d That branch of biology that deals with the mutual reactions among organisms and between organisms and their environment.

i) Amino acids ii) a catalyst iii) ecology iv) capillary water

iv Change all these definitions to the (B and C is known as A) type. Another way to define a term is very similar. We say:

A is B

or: B is known as A

or: B is called A

This is a simple expression of equivalence or identity.

Here are some examples:

a Leaching is the washing out of chemical substances from the top layer of the soil.

b Bacterial symbiosis is the relationship of mutual benefit between bacteria and plants.

Now look at this way of saying a.

a The washing out of chemical substances from the top layer of the soil is known as leaching.

You change b and c like the above.

Instead of the verb BE you have seen how we can use:

is known as

is called

may be defined as

We can also use:

B is termed A

A means B

The meaning of A is B

The definition of A is B

Write out the definitions of Ex i using the above expressions.

2 Logical connectors

a Logical sequence

Look at these sentences from the text.

In arid regions soil forming processes are largely physical. Thus, the soil closely resembles the parent rock in its chemical and mineralogical composition. In humid regions ... rock particles are strongly affected by the solvent action of water. The water may contain carbonic and other strong acids. Consequently, great changes in the physical and chemical make up of the soil take place.

THUS and CONSEQUENTLY are inter-sentential adjuncts connecting causal/resultative relationships into a logical sequence. Other words performing the same function are:

THEREFORE, SO, ACCORDINGLY, HENCE, THEN, AS A RESULT, AS A CONSEQUENCE.

Reorder the sentences below and insert a sentence adjunct, word or phrase, where appropriate.
  i There is unequal expansion and contraction of rocks.
  ii There are great daily temperature differences in sub-tropical arid regions.
  iii Physical erosion is greatest.
  b Temporal sequence
Look at these sentences from the text:

At first those cracks break huge masses of rock into large boulders. Then these are cracked into smaller boulders. Subsequently, different agents break down these rocks into finer and finer particles. The process continues till eventually small stones, gravel and sand form the basis of soil.

The words underlined connect the sentences together in a temporal sequence. Sometimes, a whole paragraph is constructed on this basis. Words that indicate temporal sequence are of three kinds:
  i At first, in the beginning, firstly, initially, to start with.
  ii Then, later on, subsequently, next, in time, afterwards.
  iii Finally, lastly, ultimately, eventually.

B STRUCTURE OF THE SENTENCE

1 Comparison
a Based on gradations
i Look at these words:
  boulders, rocks, stones, gravel, sand, silt, clay
Now compare the sizes of these particles. Use the adjective in brackets. Use the patterns (ADJ + ER), and (not as ADJ as).
a Silt and clay (fine, coarse)
b Boulders and stones (large, small)
b Based on deductions
Complete these sentences with the comparative form of an adjective (either: more/less or ADJ + ER).

Soils also vary greatly in colour. A brightly coloured soil indicates a higher degree of oxidation. So, a red soil has been .... oxidised than a black soil.

c Implied comparatives

In many passages you are likely to read there is an implied comparison. (See comprehension section, Q3, for imply-implication.) Your success in understanding the passage largely depends on your understanding what is being compared to what. These exercises will help you to do this.

i Granites and other igneous rocks are commonly grouped into acidic, intermediate and basic rocks, depending on their silica content. This may vary between 40 % for basalts, which are dark, glassy basic rocks to twice that percentage in granites.

Write 'less' or 'more' in the spaces provided:

a A granite rock contains .... silica than a basic rock.

b There is .... silica in basalt than in granite.

d Superlatives

Look at these examples:

i Instead of saying: A desert region has less rainfall than any other climatic region.

we say: A desert region has the least rainfall of any climatic region.

ii Instead of saying: More oxidation takes place in well drained soils than in any other soils.

we say: The most oxidation takes place in well drained soils.

2 *Causation*

Look at these sentences:

Instead of saying: bad drainage causes acidity we can say:

Soil acidity is $\begin{cases} \text{One} \\ \text{the result of bad drainage.} \end{cases}$

or: $\begin{cases} \text{One} \\ \text{The cause of soil acidity is bad drainage.} \end{cases}$

or: $\begin{cases} \text{One} \\ \text{The reason for soil acidity is bad drainage.} \end{cases}$

or: $\begin{cases} \text{One} \\ \text{The consequence of bad drainage is soil acidity.} \end{cases}$

or   Bad drainage results in soil acidity.

or: $\begin{cases} \text{One} \\ \text{The effect of bad drainage is soil acidity.} \end{cases}$

Note

  i *We say 'one' cause of, reason for etc. when the cause or reason we give is one among many.*

  ii *We say 'the' cause of, reason for etc. when the cause or reason we give is the only one.*

  iii *With 'result of', 'a' means the same as 'the'.*

  iv *We can say 'a cause of', 'a reason for' etc. but it's better to say 'one'.*

   Now change these sentences in the 6 ways shown above. Notice where you can say 'a', 'one' or 'the'.

a Carbonic acid causes a change in the chemical composition of rocks.

b The slow rotting of organic material causes the formation of reduced compounds.

c Intense cultivation may cause the removal of humus more rapidly than it can be replaced.

d The addition of lime causes the neutralisation of an acid soil.

e Working a clay soil while it is wet causes a loss in its aggregate structure.

f Alternate expansion and contraction causes rocks to split.

(*Note*: causes rocks to split _____ The splitting of rocks is a result of …)

Now look at these ways of expressing causation:

Intra-sentence

Adj	Noun	Verb	Connective
resultant	a	cause	because
	one cause of	result	on account of
consequent	the result of		in as much as
	the consequence of		as
	the reason for		since
	the effect of		
			due
			owing to
			so (that) (as to)

Inter-sentence

Adverb	Noun Phrase
accordingly	as a consequence

consequently	as a result
hence	as a reason for
therefore	the effect of
then	
so	
thus	

C STRUCTURE OF THE VERB PHRASE

1 The verb Be

Here are some of the patterns that the verb BE is used in:

i NP + BE + PREP PHRASE

Look at this sentence:

> Quartz crystals are in granite.

We usually say this sentence like this:

> There are quartz crystals in granite.

or Granite has quartz crystals in it.

or Granite contains quartz crystals.

or Quartz crystals exist in granite.

This is what we call the existential/locative use of the verb BE. Other verbs we may use to express this relationship include:

> find (passive)
> possess

ii NP + BE + ADJ

Look at these sentences:

> Many finely textured soils are rich in clay and organic matter.
> Water is electrically neutral.
> Most agricultural soils are acid rather than alkaline.
> Bacteria are sensitive to the pH of their environment.

We may call this the characterising or descriptive use of BE. The adjective describes a characteristic of the noun we are talking about. Notice that the adjective may be preceded by an adverb or followed by a PREP PHRASE.

Here are a few more examples:

a The number of hydrogen ions in a soil solution is usually quite small.

b Soils in arid regions are seldom acid.

iii NP$_1$ + BE + NP$_2$

Look at these examples:

> Leaching is the washing out of chemical substances from the upper layers of the soil.
> Deflocculation is the breaking up of soil aggregates.
> Aevation is the renewal of air and other gases in the soil.

There are three points to notice about these sentences:

a The subject noun is a process.
b The use of the definite article after BE.
c The predicate and subject can be reversed. In fact these sentences are typically definitions of the sort we looked at earlier in this unit. We are identifying A as B, or A + B. This is the identifying use of BE.

2 Now look at these examples:

> Superphosphate is a fertiliser.
> Rhizobium is a nitrogen fixing microbe.

When the nouns are countable we can make them plural:

> Superphosphates are fertilisers.
> Rhizobium are nitrogen fixing microbes.

What we are doing here is describing or identifying by classifying. We are saying A is a member of or can be included in a class B. We can say:

> One example of a fertiliser is superphosphate.
> One example of a crystalling rock is schist.
> One example of a substance produced by living cells is an enzyme.

3 Of course there are other kinds of relationships expressed by BE. The point is that really BE is not a verb except when it means 'something exists'. It is what we call a copulative; it joins together noun phrases or noun phrases with adjectives or preposition phrases which have a certain kind of relationship with one another, characterising, identifying, classifying.

Of course BE can have tense and an auxiliary with it.

e.g. In many parts of the tropics weathering can be extremely intense.

Another kind of relationship you must be careful of is when we mean:

> (Some) A is (some) B

For example when we say:

> Some fertilisers are salts

we mean:

> One of the characteristics of some fertilisers is that they are salts.

or   Fertilisers can be salts.

or   Fertilisers are sometimes in the form of salts.

Another example:

> The processes of erosion are largely physical.

or   Many processes of erosion are physical processes.

And what about this sentence:

> Many soils in the world are largely deficient in trace elements essential to crop growth.

Can you say what this sentence DOESN'T MEAN?

EXERCISE

i These sentences have the (verb) BE omitted. Can you put it in the correct place and in the correct form?

  a Desalinisation the removal of salts from saline soils.
  b The weathering of parent rocks only the beginning of the formation of soil.
  c Little leaching of the surface layers in desert soils.
  d Igneous rocks usually hard but they often decay.
  e An A-horizon, rich in organic matter and weathered materials, commonly dark in colour.
  f All manner of materials in the earth's rock crust.
  g Some soils a fraction of an inch thick, others several feet deep (2 BE's).
  h Calcium and magnesium two of the essential nutrient elements to plants.
  i Saline soils halomorphic soils.

ii What kind of relationship does BE express?

iii Rewrite the following sentences using these verbal expressions instead of BE:

  a a) above: can be defined as
  b b) above: exist
  c c) above: occur

d c) above: can be found
e c) above: have
f f) above: there are
g f) above: are to be found
h i) above: may be classified as

REFERENCES

1 Halliday, M. A. K., 'Existing Research and Future Work', in *Languages for Special Purposes*, CILT Reports and Paper No. 1, CILT, 1969.
2 Huddleston, R. A., Hudson, R. A., Winter, E. O., and Henrici, A., *Sentence and Clause in Scientific English*, 1968.
3 James, C. V., 'A Note on Language Skills', in CILT Reports and Papers No. 8, September, 1972.
4 Harré, R., *An Introduction to the Logic of the Sciences*, Macmillan, 1967.
5 Widdowson, H. G., 'The Teaching of Rhetoric to Students of Science and Technology,' CILT Reports and Papers No. 7, October, 1971. See also Chapter 3 of this volume.
6 Hasan, R., 'Grammatical Cohesion in Spoken and Written English', Paper 7 in *Programme in Linguistics and English Teaching*, Longman, 1968.

8

Designing a Course in Advanced Listening Comprehension

J. MORRISON

1 Teaching Situation

1.1 *Students*

Each year, in common with other British universities, the University of Newcastle upon Tyne receives students from overseas for postgraduate study in sciences and science-related subjects such as forestry, agriculture, engineering.

The command of English possessed by these students varies enormously. It *is* safe to say, however, that their reading skills are likely to be better than their listening skills, because even among those who have had extensive exposure to spoken English (and they are likely to be a minority) it has not usually been to British English spoken by a native-speaker. Further, those students who have studied English and possess a formal qualification in it (such as a School Certificate) are liable to find that this does not equip them to follow spoken English in learning situations with native-speaking lecturers where no linguistic concessions are made to the presence in the audience of what may well be a single overseas student. (If the reader imagines himself, with School Certificate French, having to follow a lecture on advanced arboricultural economy in a provincial French university, it will help him to appreciate the situation.) From the teacher's point of view, these students have only two things in common – their orientation towards scientific disciplines and their need to improve their listening skills. What they do *not* have in common can effectively be illustrated by the following figures, which relate to the University of Newcastle upon Tyne for the academic year 1973–74. The population of overseas students in their first year of postgraduate studies in sciences consisted of 86 students, who represented:

26 mother-tongues

33 university departments
36 students without any formal qualification in English
an age-range from 22–38.

Of these, 51 were pursuing M.Sc. courses, 15 Ph.D. courses and the remainder M.Phil. or Diploma courses.

1.2 *Teaching Problems*

English is not what these students have come to study. As specialist postgraduate students, few are prepared to devote a great deal of time, even if they could afford it, to the formal study of English. Attendance at remedial English classes is rarely insisted on by the host department, and then only when a student is very clearly in trouble because of his inadequate command of English. Their physical dispersal throughout the university makes it virtually impossible to organise them as a class within a normal teaching timetable. The commercial tapes available in the Language Centre for private practice and drills, however useful for 'social' English, are too 'structural' in approach to be of much help in their immediate need as postgraduate students – that is, in helping them to follow their lectures. (This may be one explanation of why, in the population referred to, only 27 out of the 86 students claimed to make use of the Language Centre tapes for private practice.) The need, then, is for teaching and practice materials which the student can recognise as relevant to his needs and effective in alleviating his difficulties. Otherwise, in a voluntary situation and probably involving attendance in the evening, he simply won't come.

The problem for the teacher may be summarised as follows:

(a) to identify the type of spoken English which, for this student, exemplifies his chief learning-situations – i.e. identifying *relevant discourse*;

(b) to identify within such discourse the features of English which are most persistent in causing him difficulty – i.e. *features of persistent difficulty*.

(c) to design materials which will, within samples of relevant discourse, enable features of persistent difficulty to be exploited for listening comprehension and practice, and in the course of which exposure to spoken discourse will be maximised in a meaningful way.

2 Applied Research

2.1 *Listening Situations and Relevant Discourse*

The assumption has sometimes been too readily made that what the overseas student needs to master for listening-comprehension is the English of what Chaplen[1] calls a 'well-prepared University lecture'. Observation of students in their learning-situations suggested that for these postgraduates the commonest situation was not the formal university lecture at all, but that it was represented by a smaller group on more intimate terms with the lecturer who, although what he said was high in informational content, spoke in an informal register quite different – especially in the way in which ideas and arguments are connected – from the written English which, according to Chaplen, is 'the basis of many well-prepared University lectures' and which Abercrombie designates 'spoken prose'.[2] A questionnaire revealed that the listening-situations to which the students were exposed could be defined as:

> formal lectures
> informal lectures
> seminars/tutorials
> individual discussions

It also revealed that, in order of frequency and order of difficulty in understanding, seminars/tutorials and informal lectures came first and second – a result which was confirmed by a listening-comprehension test based on these situations. Furthermore, it emerged that, although the order of difficulty remained the same among the more able and the less able students, among the more able there was considerably less difference in performance between one situation and another than there was among the less able. What this means is that the listening-situation is itself important *as a factor in comprehension* in direct relation to the student's listening ability. The implication for practice materials is that the discourse-material should exemplify the language of the seminar/tutorial or informal lecture situation – that is, should *not* be based on written sources but should – while high in informational content – exhibit the features of a genuine spoken register, as against the 'spoken prose' of the formal lecture.

2.2 *Features of Persistent Difficulty*

Before discussion of these, a brief note on the method used to identify them is necessary. A listening-comprehension test based on videotaped samples of the main listening-situations was administered to three groups. The first group consisted of overseas students at the end of their first year of postgraduate studies, that is, after considerable exposure; the second group, very similar in composition, were students at the beginning of their first year of postgraduate study, that is, after minimal exposure; the third, Control, group consisted of native speakers. The linguistic features tested in the questions were based on the writer's teaching experience, on discussion with and observation of students, on students' responses to a questionnaire, and on the results of a pilot test.

The features of persistent difficulty were identified thus. First, questions which discriminated effectively between native-speakers and the first (post-exposure) group of postgraduates were identified, and the process was repeated with the second (pre-exposure) group. Next, among these questions, the ones which discriminated effectively between the second (pre-exposure) group and the first (post-exposure) group were identified. By this means, a distinction could be drawn between features which – while difficult for *all* non-native speakers – are features of difficulty chiefly initially, and those which persist in causing difficulty. Thus for example, as might be expected, vocabulary emerged as a main difficulty on arrival but after a year's exposure had a much lower status as a problem feature – except for nominalised groups (e.g. life support systems) which are of course quite frequent in scientific discourse.

The features of persistent difficulty arrived at were, in this order: logical connectors, phonology, referential items, nominalised groups, idiom, vocabulary. Obviously, this list has no pretensions to being exhaustive or to accounting for *all* features of difficulty in the type of spoken discourse with which these students are concerned. But what *can* be said is that the features here identified *are* a source of difficulty, and are therefore worth stressing in practice material for listening-comprehension. The importance of being able to handle logical connectors (e.g. *so that*, *thus*, *consequently*) and referential items (e.g. *this* means ..., *what* I've said ..., *which* implies ... and other items of anaphora, and cataphora) for following continuous discourse clearly emerged. Obviously, such features can only be practised *in* continuous discourse – material at the sentence level is of little value. The same applies to phonological features such as connective or contrastive stress, or the drop in pitch and increase in pace which signal the vocal equivalent of parentheses. Therefore, the features identified as important clearly have implications for the type of practice material that will be appropriate.

3 Preparation of the Course

3.1 *Discourse Element*

The problem for the teacher, bearing in mind the type of discourse which is relevant and the features of such discourse which are important, is to provide structured listening practice, with a twofold aim. First, it must provide practice in the sense of increased, intensified and controlled *exposure* to appropriate discourse material; second, it must give practice in the sense of *exercises* which will help to reinforce listening-comprehension skills by concentrating on features of importance. This has been well summarised as the problem of 'how to make "usable learning instruments" from "unedited texts in the target language which contain in natural form the important, frequent and useful phonological, lexical and grammatical elements of the target language". In other words, any persistent inability to perform ... will best be eradicated while attending to a variety of natural, contextual samples of language use.'[3]

In these 'natural, contextual samples' of genuine spoken discourse, the speaker in developing an argument typically indulges in re-phrasings, incomplete structures; he varies his pace and pitch, he employs grammatical intonation and stress; his use of idiom (e.g. what I'm getting at here ...) is untypical of 'spoken prose', as is his use of logical connectors and referential items. Further, the fact that the *argument* is often pre-structured (in the form of notes, points to be covered) means that the rate of delivery is faster and the redundancy lesser than is the case in genuinely impromptu speech.

For the discourse-element of the practice-material, it was considered that excerpts from genuine university seminars or informal lectures were too highly subject-specific to offer infor-mational appeal to students. However, a useful source of material was identified in radio broadcast discussions on science-orientated topics – preferably the type of interview with an expert who, in response to questions, does most of the talking on a topic on which he is able to speak fluently and authoritatively. (A sample is given in the final section.)

3.2 *Practice Exercises*

These must be designed to give the student practice in coping with the features of persistent difficulty *in relation to a meaningful context*. Within such a context, they are designed to do three things:

(a) to increase command of lexis, with special attention to such features as nominalised groups and idiom;
(b) to develop ability to cope with the referential system – that is, with the cohesive devices, grammatical and lexical, in spoken discourse;
(c) to improve ability to recognise the significant elements in the sound system of spoken discourse – such as the phonological cohesive devices characteristic of spoken discourse like contrastive and connective stress, and pitch and intonation (e.g. the intonation of doubt).

Where possible, all of these aims should be reinforced in exercise-exploitation of the important features. Thus, a nominalised group such as 'smoke emission control' might be required to be chosen or explained with regard to *meaning* in one exercise, to be identified as the *referent* of 'this' in another, and to be distinguished from 'smoky machine control' in a *sound*-exercise.

Obviously, the use of 'unedited texts' for the discourse element does impose a limitation in that the linguistic features requiring attention are initially presented only through those examples of such features as arise in the discourse – but of course this need not mean that teaching is restricted to these items. Thus, if in the discourse the logical connector 'that is' occurs, the teacher can then – at the appropriate time – offer alternatives to be substituted (e.g. *namely, which is to say, in other words*). The essential point is that initial attention is given to the item *in its communicative context* and substitutions are also made within that context. Basing the lesson on an 'unedited' text, therefore, is not necessarily a constraint on the *coverage* of important linguistic features, only on the order of initial presentation.

The basic principle in the design of the exercises is to avoid an approach-by-classification – that is, by extracting from the discourse those features requiring attention and treating them in exercises or drills divorced from their communicative context. Since in listening-comprehension a set of complex perceptive skills is involved, a drill-approach in which these skills are broken down and practised in isolation is considered unlikely to be effective for two reasons. First, the element of complexity-in-use is eliminated – so what is being practised lacks reality. Second, and in my opinion more important, in a drill approach the informational content is almost invariably trivial – so what is being practised lacks relevance. In listening comprehension work at an advanced level, the student's concern is to improve his performance *in the reception of information* through exercise of the perceptive skills – material with a trivial informational content therefore has low value both as practice material and for motivation. For these students, then, the practice material must offer real information in genuine purposive discourse.

3.3 *Exemplification: Sample Course Material*

The unit given at the end of this section provides work for two one-hour sessions. It can be used with a teacher in a language laboratory, or by a student working alone with a tape recorder. Either procedure should promote the basic aims, of maximising exposure to appropriate discourse in a meaningful way and of giving practice in coping with the features of importance. The assistance of a teacher will clearly increase coverage of such features, but the main feature of the exercises is that, even in the absence of a teacher, the student is forced to listen to meaningful connected discourse in completing them.(The reader may find it preferable to study the sample material, – pp. 169–177 – before reading the account of procedure, below.)

   The procedure is as follows:

SESSION 1

Stage 1: the student hears the discourse element in its entirety. It lasts about five minutes.

Stage 2: the discourse element is repeated. At intervals, a 'ping' is heard and the student is directed to answer a question on his worksheet. After a pause for the student to answer, when the discourse recommences it has gone back to include the portion relevant to the question that has just been asked. The questions in this stage, under the heading of 'Understanding' cover lexis, idiom, structures, allusion, implication. For example, for question 3 of Exercise 1, the 'ping' occurs after the words 'wind and water power again become competitive'; when the tape restarts after the pause, it starts at 'And coupled with advances in other fields ...' so that the student hears again 'And coupled with advances in other fields (the very low friction bearing, for example, another point of space spin-off) wind and water power again become competitive.' The student is able immediately to check his comprehension in this way for many of the items.

Stage 3: excerpts from the discourse element are heard. These are heard twice – once before the student makes his response, and once after. They cover aspects of phonology – assimilation, reduction, stress, pitch, intonation. Since it is the *sound* that is the principal concern in these exercises rather than the information (although, as explained, they also have the function of reinforcement of other aspects) the excerpts are grouped together after the continuous discourse for convenience, so that examples of the sound-pattern in question may be concentrated for listening-practice without the need to spend time re-locating the occurrences in the main body of discourse – the point is, of course, that all the occurrences, as the student can see, *do* have a communicative function *in* the discourse.

Stage 4: the complete discourse element is heard again and at each 'ping' the correct response for Stage 2 is given. If it is being handled by a teacher, this is the appropriate time to make teaching points on alternative or equivalent structures or expressions. Students note errors on their work-sheets for corrective practice in Stage 5. The correct responses for Stage 3 are also given.

Stage 5: the student listens to the complete discourse element while following it on a transcript, *which must not be used until this stage.* He can then refer visually to any part of the discourse, checking the sound against the transcript, re-listening as often as he wishes to points which he finds difficult or where his response was wrong. He can also practise imitating the speech, if he finds this helpful.

SESSION 2

Stage 6: the student hears the complete discourse element.

Stage 7: the discourse element is repeated, with 'pings'. This time, the questions deal with items of cohesion, requiring for example a referent to be given. (The exercise is designated 'Connection'.) Again, where practicable, on re-starting, the tape has gone back to include the portion relevant to the question that has just been answered.

Stage 8: as for Stage 4 (correction, teaching points).

Stage 9: the student is required *by listening to the discourse* to answer general comprehension questions or to make brief notes on specific points.

Stage 10: as for Stage 5. (i.e. the student can measure his performance against the transcript, and practise where he needs it.)

Sample Unit

(Discourse element from a radio broadcast.)

VOICE 1   Power from water – running water and the tides – has so far been exploited amazingly little. And if wind power seems too naive, Geoffrey Pardoe's colleagues built a large windmill a few years ago based on advanced aerodynamics learned from propellor design. And coupled with advances in other fields (the very low friction bearing, for example, another point of space spin-off) wind and water power again become competitive. They're free; they're clean (that is, pollution-free); and they can be small and localised.

Going to the sub-tropics, there are experimental rigs in operation now which are using the difference between the deep-sea and the surface temperature as a kind of motor to start a power cycle. Isn't this a typical example of the way we should be exploring possibilities?

VOICE 2   Yes. I'm sure this is the right sort of thinking. Em – any phenomenon – be it a change of light levels or temperature levels – anything which em can with our knowledge be used to convert eh one form of energy gradient to another (which produces for example electricity) I think should be explored; eh, I'm sure we can turn our experience eh with ingenuity into a variety of ways. Whether or not em it's practical to use what must be a fairly small temperature gradient in this way I would not like to say, I don't think I'm in a position to comment in depth. But on the principle, yes I'm sure we should em explore all sorts of possibilities for this form of energy harnessing.

VOICE 1   A somewhat grandiose notion (partly inspired by the success of liquid hydrogen as a rocket fuel) is to produce hydrogen by electrolysing sea-water in an offshore nuclear plant, to pipe it ashore, and use it as a substitute for gas or petrol. Geoffrey Pardoe's comment was that handling liquid hydrogen, and the problems of the very low temperatures involved, don't as yet really lend themselves to operations on a large scale or by other than very skilled technicians. But you've forgotten something, you say – whatever happened to nuclear energy? Simply, nuclear power twenty years ago was over-sold. The enthusiasts hadn't quite reckoned on the time and cash needed to produce a commercial unit – and above all they had to stop and develop suitable metals and minerals from which to fabricate the reactor and its components. Now, with the Advanced Gas-Cooled Reactors and the

Prototype Fast Breeder building, the nuclear industry is, in its own jargon, 'coming on steam' – and nuclear energy was last year the cheapest we bought. If you imagine, by the way, that a reactor is a kind of bomb in a concrete chamber, it's not – it's a long, slow burn. Which is the prime problem about the next move, energy from fusion or welding atoms together, instead of from splitting them or fission. The temperature of the reaction is too high, and the key to the Slow Burn hasn't yet been found. But clearly, the second chapter in the nuclear story is about to open and with the opening phases too of solar energy and the others, the world energy story of the twenty-first century is well under way.

VOICE 3 Well, when we get that extra energy – if we do – it'll come in useful as a power supply.

Sample Unit Student's Worksheet

Vocabulary and idiom (*as used in this talk*)
coupled with: considered together with
spin-off: in technology, an advantage or development apart from the one originally intended (a kind of scientific side-effect)
a phenomenon: any natural occurrence
ingenuity: mental adaptability or originality
grandiose: very ambitious
to fabricate: to make or build
jargon: the special language of a particular science
the prime problem: the main difficulty

LISTEN CAREFULLY FOR THESE GROUPS IN THE TALK:
propellor design: the design of propellors
very low friction bearing: a bearing which produces a small amount of friction
energy-harnessing: the process of harnessing (making use of) energy
offshore nuclear plant: a factory operated by nuclear power and located at sea
Advanced Gas-Cooled Reactor⎫
Prototype Fast Breeder　　　⎬ types of nuclear power plants

SESSION 1

Exercise 1 Understanding
1 (a) What two kinds of water does he suggest could be used to

generate power:
ANSWER i ....
         ii ....
  (b) Very little use has been made of water power, in the speaker's
      opinion.
                                         TRUE/FALSE

2 Modern technology cannot be applied to wind power.
                                         TRUE/FALSE

3 (a) What example of a spin-off from space technology will help to
      make wind and water power competitive?
      ANSWER ....
  (b) *competitive* as used here means:
      A worthwhile in economic terms
      B efficient in engineering terms
                                 ANSWER ....

4 Give *two* advantages of wind and water power
   ANSWER i they are ....
           ii they are ....

5 The difference between the temperature deep in the sea and the
   temperature at the sea's surface is being used:
      A commercially
      B experimentally   ANSWER ....

6 ... *be it* a change of light levels or temperature levels ... *be it*
   means:
      A because it is
      B although it is
      C whether it is   ANSWER ....

7 ... a fairly small temperature gradient
   Instead of *fairly small* you could say:
      A very small
      B reasonably small
      C rather small   ANSWER ....

8 Theoretically, liquid hydrogen could be made from sea-water for
   use in place of petrol and gas.
                                         TRUE/FALSE

9 There are no serious problems in handling liquid hydrogen.
                                         TRUE/FALSE

10 What two factors were not sufficiently considered by the enthusiasts for nuclear energy?
ANSWER i the .... needed
ii the .... needed

11 More important than either of the two factors mentioned in question 10, what did the nuclear energy enthusiasts have to develop?
ANSWER They had to develop suitable ....
....

12 In the jargon of the nuclear industry, *'coming on stream'* must mean:
A becoming active
B utilising more water
C proceeding very fast   ANSWER ....

13 What is *fusion*?
ANSWER Fusion is ....
What is *fission*?
ANSWER Fission is ....

14 The *key to the Slow Burn* means a method of maintaining a low enough temperature during reaction.
TRUE/FALSE/NOT STATED

15 What is *solar energy*?
ANSWER It is ....

Exercise 2 Listening
Look at the extracts. Listen to them. Fill in the blanks.
1 Going .... sub-tropics .... experimental rigs .... operation
2 using .... difference .... deep sea ....
surface temperatures
3 a typical example .... way ....
exploring possibilities
4 electrolysing sea water is an ....
5 Now with the .... and the ....
... . building
6 it's not – it's a ....

Exercise 3 Idiom
Look at the extracts. Listen to them, looking out for the words that are in italics.

1 whether or not em it's practical to use *what must be* a fairly small temperature gradient in this way *I would not like to say*

    (a) *what must be* means (choose *two*):

    A   something which has a duty to be

    B   something which obviously is

    C   something which is necessarily

    D   something which can be

                                 ANSWERS ....

    (b) *I would not like to say* means:

    A   I am unwilling to discuss it

    B   I have no opinion

    C   I am not sure   ANSWER ....

2 ... handling liquid hydrogen, and the problems of the very low temperatures involved *don't as yet lend themselves* to operations
The words in italics mean:

    A   up until now they are not suitable

    B   up until now we have not been allowed to use them

                                 ANSWER ....

3 the enthusiasts *hadn't quite reckoned* on the time and cash needed to produce a commercial unit
The words in italics mean:

    A   they had not believed how much would be needed

    B   they had paid insufficient attention to how much would be needed

    C   they had not calculated how much would be needed

                                 ANSWER ....

4 But clearly, the *second chapter* in the nuclear *story* is about to open and with the *opening phrases* too of solar energy the world energy *story* is *well under way*.

    (a) the speaker compares energy development to a book (using terms like *second chapter*, *opening phrases*, and *story*). Write down the 'book-expression' used by him which you think means the same as:

    A   the earliest stages ....

    B   The next development ....

    C   A full account of the world energy situation ....

    ....

    (b) *well under way* means:

    A   proceeding satisfactorily

B   a long way below what is needed

ANSWER ....

Exercise 4   Stress

Look at the extracts. Listen for the words in italics.

1 Power from water – running water and the tides – has so far been exploited amazingly little. And if *wind* power seems too naive, Geoffrey Pardoe's colleagues built a *large* windmill ...

Fill in the blanks:

A   *wind* is stressed in order to signal a shift of topic from .... power.

B   *large* is stressed in answer to the possible (unspoken) objection that only .... windmills would be practicable.

2 whether or not em it's practical to use what must be a fairly small temperature gradient in this way I would not like to say, I don't think I'm in a position to comment in depth. But on the *principle*, yes I'm sure we should em explore all sorts of possibilities.

Underline the word *earlier in this extract* with which the speaker expects you to contrast *principle*.

3 *any* phenomenon – be it a change of light levels or temperature-levels – anything which can with our knowledge be used ... by stressing *any*, he is making clear that he means:

A   any *single* phenomenon

B   any *type* of phenomenon

ANSWER ....

4 ... and the problems of the very low temperatures involved don't as yet really lend themselves to operations on a *large* scale.

The stress on *large* suggests that small-scale operations are already practicable.

TRUE/FALSE

5 ... the enthusiasts hadn't *quite* reckoned on the time and cash needed ...

The stress on *quite* suggests:

A   they had paid *some* attention, but not enough

B   they had paid absolutely *no* attention

ANSWER ....

SESSION 2

Exercise 5   Reference

1 ... *they* can be small and localised
   To what does *they* refer?
   ANSWER *They* refers to ....

2 Isn't *this* a typical example of the way that we should be exploring
   possibilities?
   (a) To what does *this* refer?
       ANSWER...
   (b) *possibilities* of what?
       ANSWER of ....

3 ... a variety of *ways*
   ways of doing what?
   ANSWER ways of...

4 ... what must be a fairly small temperature gradient
   FILL IN THE BLANKS
   These words refer to the difference between .... and ....
   temperatures in the ....

5 ... but on the *principle*, yes
   To what principle is he referring?
   ANSWER to the principle that we should ....
   ....

6 ... and use *it* as a substitute for gas and petrol
   To what does *it* refer?
   ANSWER to ....

7 ... or by other than very skilled technicians
   He means:
   A not only by skilled technicians
   B except by skilled technicians
                                                    ANSWER ....

8 ... the enthusiasts hadn't quite reckoned
   The *enthusiasts* referred to are the people who (ANSWER) ......
   ....

9 ... to produce a commercial unit
   a *commercial unit* for what purpose?
   ANSWER A commercial unit to ....

10 ... *it*'s not – *it*'s a long, slow burn
    To what does each *it* refer?
    ANSWER to ....

11 it's not – it's a long, slow burn. Which is the prime problem about the next move, energy from fusion or welding atoms together, instead of from splitting them or fission. The temperature of the reaction is too high, and the key to the Slow Burn hasn't yet been found.

(a) *which is the prime problem*: these words refer to:
   A slow burn
   B fission   ANSWER ....

(b) The *next move* is:
   A fission
   B fusion   ANSWER ....

(c) The Slow Burn refers to the required temperature during the reaction

                                    TRUE/FALSE/NOT STATED

12 ... of solar energy and the others
   Apart from solar energy and nuclear energy, what *others* have been mentioned? Give *two*.
   ANSWER i ....
           ii ....

Exercise 6 Pitch
Listen carefully to the extract. Try to listen for a slight drop in the pitch, with sometimes a slight increase in speed. *Underline* the main part of the message, and put *brackets* ( ) round the 'extra' or 'aside' part of the message.

1 and coupled with advances in other fields the very low friction bearing for example another point of space spin-off wind and water power again become competitive

2 they're free they're clean that is pollution-free and they can be small and localised

3 anything which em can with our knowledge be used to convert eh one form of energy gradient to another which produces for example electricity I think should be explored

4 A somewhat grandiose notion partly inspired by the success of liquid hydrogen as a rocket fuel is to produce hydrogen by electrolysing sea-water in an offshore nuclear plant

Exercise 7
Try to answer these questions by listening to the talk. Do not refer to the transcript or to the answers over the page unless repeated listening fails to yield the answer.

1 What item of spin off from space technology does the speaker think will help to make wind and water power commercially practicable?

2 Where are experiments to utilise temperature differences in sea water being carried out?

3 Summarise the proposal for producing hydrogen by electrolysing sea water – include the difficulties in your answer.

4 What factors had the enthusiasts for nuclear power not given sufficient attention to?

5 Name the two types of nuclear power plant which are now being built.

6 What basically is meant by 'the key to the Slow Burn'?

Answers
1 the low friction bearing

2 in the sub-tropics

3 make it in offshore nuclear plants
pipe it ashore
substitute for gas or petrol
problems
very low temperatures
need for highly skilled technicians

4 the time and cash needed
the need to develop new materials and minerals

5 Advanced Gas-Cooled Reactor
Prototype Fast Breeder

6 a means of controlling the temperature during the fusion reaction

REFERENCES

1 Chaplen, E. F., 'The Identification of Non-native Speakers of English Likely to Underachieve in University Courses through Inadequate Command of the Language', (Ph.D. Thesis Manchester University), 1970, p. 115.
2 Abercrombie, D., *Studies in Phonetics and Linguistics*. OUP, 1965, pp. 2–5.
3 Reibel, D. A., 'Language Learning Analysis', IRAL, Vol. 7, No. 4, p. 292 quoted by Standish, P. 'Towards a strategy for advanced language learning', AVLA, Vol. 10, No. 3, pp. 141–144.

9

Language Practice Materials for Economists

R. R. JORDAN

1 Background

At the University of Manchester special classes in English are arranged for overseas postgraduate students in need of such help to follow courses in their specialist subjects. Multiple-choice speeded grammar and vocabulary tests, followed by an interview, plus information from the students, are used to determine if help is needed. The students requiring most help are usually those attending a one-year Diploma or Master's degree course which is examinable. Such courses generally consist of numerous lectures, practical and/or seminars; a number of essays or reports are expected during the year. At the end of the third term an examination is set consisting, traditionally, of 3-hour question papers. Examples of these courses at Manchester are the Diploma course in Economic Development and the M.A. course in Economics or Econometrics.

The students from these courses who attend the voluntary English classes are predominantly speakers of Spanish (Latin America), Arabic, Farsi (Iran), and Greek. Normally twelve attend the Diploma English classes and ten the M.A. English classes for two hours a week of classes plus, on average, a further two hours a week using self-instructional material in the language laboratory in their free time. Timetabling is usually a difficulty with postgraduates following a variety of courses; however, in this case, cooperation with the Department of Economics has been close and timetables arranged with a minimum of difficulty. Departmental cooperation is essential for any specialist subject classes.

2 Initial Problems

2.1 Skills

The students have a knowledge of economics, already possessing a

179

first degree in economics or a related subject. However, most of them have not used English to obtain their degree, except in the matter of reading some textbooks in English. What, then, are their basic language problems on arrival in Manchester? These are listed below according to skills.

1 Inability to understand spoken English when delivered at a normal native-speaker rate. This is especially true when the language is informal or colloquial. Research has been conducted into this by J. W. Morrison (M.Ed. 1974, University of Newcastle upon Tyne: 'An Investigation of Problems in Listening-Comprehension encountered by Overseas Students in the First Year of Postgraduate Studies in Sciences in the University of Newcastle upon Tyne, and the Implications for Teaching'); informal lectures and seminars were found to cause the most difficulty. The difficulty of colloquial language in lectures has also been investigated by C. D. Holes (M.A. 1972, University of Birmingham: 'An Investigation into some aspects of the English language problems of two groups of overseas postgraduate students at Birmingham University'). Aspects of listening difficulties are:

(a) Inability to focus attention on details and overall meaning.
(b) Inability to understand, recognise or distinguish: unstressed syllables, contractions, negatives, plurality, some verb forms, figures.
(c) Recognition (and also own pronunciation) of economic terminology i.e. problems of sound/spelling relationships – often the word is recognised in print but not in speech. This is particularly true of formulae and other numerical expressions used in statistics and econometrics.

2 Inability to take notes in English while listening to a lecture.
3 Inability to express self coherently or fluently in speech and a consequent inability to take an active role in seminars. Generally, there is a lack of self-confidence and of opportunity for practice.
4 Inability to write academic prose; a tendency to confuse styles e.g. mixing informal speech with formal writing.

2.2 *Language Features*

Which language features are selected for inclusion in the material used to practise the skills referred to above? Ideally, the selection would be based upon linguistic analysis of economics lectures, seminars and texts (displaying frequency of occurrence and categorisation of items in the different modes) tested with students to reveal items of difficulty. Frequency of occurrence in itself does not represent difficulty, as redundancy may operate, but it is a reasonable basis from which to commence. Sometimes linguistic analyses exist: Wijasuriya, B.S. (M.Ed. 1971, University of Manchester: 'The Occurrence of Discourse-markers and Inter-sentence Connectives in University Lectures and their Place in the Testing and Teaching of Listening Comprehension in English as a Foreign Language'); Sim, D. D. (M.Ed. 1974, University of Manchester: 'Grammatical Cohesion in English and Advanced Reading Comprehension for Overseas Students'); Tinkler, T. C. (M.Ed. 1973, University of Manchester: 'The Use of the Passive in Certain Social Science Lectures, and Implications for Teaching English to Non-native Speakers').

When the analysis does not exist, and usually it does not for reasons of time and conflicting priorities, then a list of items causing difficulty has to be drawn up from observation, teaching experience and testing. Initially, items are selected for practice without which there would be interference in communication. In addition, important features of academic discourse are included as this is the operating mode for the students viz. style, logical connectives and the language of caution and approximation.

Linguistic analyses, observation, teaching experience and testing indicate that some of the language features occurring most frequently and/or causing most difficulty for students of economics are:

1 conditionals, passives; present simple tense ('stem + s')
2 modifiers; qualifiers
3 logical connectives
4 relative clauses
5 comparison and contrast
6 sufficiency and insufficiency (and excess)
7 figures

These are in addition to others indicated above, e.g. contractions, negatives and plurality.

3 Material and Use

With an indication of the language features and skills to be practised and developed, the question of type of material and method of use arises. After trial and error it was found that the postgraduate economics students were more highly motivated by material that was directly related to or actually used in their course of studies. Thus for the Diploma students considerable use is made of the basic coursebook *Leading Issues in Economic Development* by G. M. Meier (OUP 2nd edition 1970), and for the M.A. students articles in *Monetary Theory* edited by R. W. Clower (Penguin Modern Economics Readings). The Departments cooperated by providing recommended reading lists, suggesting priority topics and reading, and enabling a number of lectures to be taped; sample examination questions were also provided in the second term for practice purposes. The bulk of the material used is authentic from the point of view of the academic language and economics content: the appeal to the students is that they are learning about the subject matter, or at least revising it, at the same time as they are practising the language.

Having obtained a quantity of source material, it then had to be divided into units that were better suited for use in the classroom with a teacher and units that could be utilised in the language laboratory as self-instructional material (tapes, instruction sheet, worksheets, answer sheets and texts). Exercises had to be constructed to practise the language features referred to above and at the same time to develop the skills found to be in need of development. An outline summary is given below.

Mini-lectures were composed to assist listening comprehension: guided note-taking sheets were provided; blank-filling sheets were devised to focus attention on specific language features and economics terminology. Question sheets were constructed which required answers in figures from information in the talks; a map of the U.K. was duplicated upon which features had to be marked based upon a description given in a talk. Worksheets were produced which asked questions focussing attention on the economics content of a talk; others reproduced jumbled parts of sentences from the talk which then had to be written out in full. Mathematical expressions were taped, reproduced in figures and also in words. Formal, written economics definitions and descriptions were reproduced in the informal, spoken mode: these were then studied and contrasted. Eventually, the students were required to listen to informal descriptions and, after taking notes, reproduce them in the formal written mode. Definite statements from economics books were compared to similar but cautious statements and the language features noted: the students were required to transform the sentences both ways. A passage was studied which developed an argument; the use of the connectives was noted; parallel or similar passages were constructed with blanks standing for the connectives. Segmental diagrams and tabular information for different years were compared and contrasted.

At a more advanced level, later in the course, the students were required to listen to parts of full-length taped lectures, focussing upon some language features and upon comprehension. The lectures were those recorded in the Departments; additionally, some from radio or television were made use of: sometimes recorded direct, sometimes reproduced by means of the text published in *The Listener* (e.g. 'The Case Against Foreign Aid' by Professor Peter Bauer, from the BBC 2 TV programme 'Controversy', published in *The Listener* on 21st September, 1972). Some Open University broadcasts are very suitable; video-tape recordings could be invaluable but in this case have not been experimented with.

Initially, the English classes concentrate in the first term on listening and the associated difficulties, together with taking notes. There is also emphasis on the recognition and pronunciation of lexis. This is developed during the second term but more emphasis is placed upon the ability to discuss, give very short talks, and to write on economics topics (later, timed to simulate examination conditions). Generally, the most difficult situation for the students, and the one most difficult to guide, is the simulated seminar or discussion: the most able students try to contribute, while those with most language difficulties hold back, often too self-conscious or ashamed to display their difficulties. Patient questioning and prior preparation by the student can help, but it still remains, in many ways, unsatisfactory.

4 Sample Material

4.1 The first two paragraphs of an introductory talk on British Agriculture (total length about 1,000 words).

'Let us now look at agriculture. As I expect you are all aware, Britain is a densely populated, industrialised country relying on imports for nearly half of its food supply. By the way, it's as well to remember that the density of population is one of the highest in the world. In Britain as a whole, there were 592 people per square mile in 1972; in England alone there were 920. This compares with 977 in the Netherlands, 819 in Belgium and 724 in Japan.

'To return to the point we were considering – food supply. We could put the emphasis the other way and say that Britain now produces just over half of its total food requirements or two-thirds of all that can be grown in our temperate climate. Although nearly half of our food supply is imported, agriculture is one of this country's largest and most important industries. It employs 651,000 people – in other words, $2\frac{1}{2}$ per cent of the total working population – and provides about 2.8 per cent of the gross national product. Putting this rather crudely, we can say that $2\frac{1}{2}$ per cent of the working population provide enough food for just over half the total population of the country. This would seem to suggest that the industry is very efficient, achieving high productivity with perhaps a large degree of mechanisation.'

Exercises (samples)

(1) Blank-filling: concentrating upon modifiers. The sentences occur in sequence in the talk. The talk is listened to a second time and the words written in (those in italics are the ones omitted).

1 Britain is a *densely* populated, industrialised country.

2 The industry is very efficient, achieving *high* productivity with perhaps a *large* degree of mechanisation.

3 Milk and egg yields have also risen *considerably*.

4 All of this *increased* output has been achieved with a declining labour force.

5 Labour productivity has increased *significantly*.

6 *Considerable* capital has been invested and Britain has today one of the most *highly* mechanised farming industries in the world.

(2) Questions to practise the quick understanding of numbers and the ability to write them quickly. (The answers are given here.)

1 What was the density of population per square mile in England in 1972?   920

2 What was the density of population per square mile in Belgium?   819

3 What proportion of its food requirements does Britain produce itself?   just over half

4 How many people are employed in agriculture?   651,000

5 What percentage of the working population is employed in agriculture? $2\frac{1}{2}\%$

(3) Note-taking for the first two paragraphs: the kinds of

abbreviations used and possible notes.

G.B. = densely pop. – 592 per sq. m. (E = 920)
     imports c. $\frac{1}{2}$ food
     but agri. = large & imp. ind.
     employs 651,000 i.e. $2\frac{1}{2}$ % work. pop.
     provides 2.8 % G.N.P.
ind. = v. eff. ? – *high prod.* & mechan. ?

(4) Sentences for repetition; they can also be used afterwards for dictation purposes; the complete exercise provides a summary of the talk.

1 Britain is a densely populated, industrialised country.

2 The density of population is one of the highest in the world.

3 There were 592 people per square mile in 1972.

4 Agriculture is one of this country's largest and most important industries.

5 It employs 651,000 people, in other words, $2\frac{1}{2}$ per cent of the total working population.

6 The industry is very efficient.

4.2 A blank-filling, listening exercise based on a talk (consisting of an article reproduced on tape: 'The Neutrality of Money in Comparative Statistics and Growth' by A. L. Marty in *Monetary Theory* edited by R. W. Clower; Penguin Modern Economics Readings). The words in italics are those omitted; this exercise concentrates on the use of the present simple active and passive verb tenses.

The recent volume by Gurley and Shaw *presents* a theory of the role of financial institutions in a growing economy. A neo-classical world *is assumed* in which prices *are* flexible, employment *is* full, and money illusion *is* absent. The author's procedure *is* to begin with a rudimentary economy which *contains* only one financial market, that for money, and one financial institution, the government monetary system. Their second model *adds* a financial market for homogeneous business bonds, *issued by* private firms, which *are purchased by* both the government banking system and the public. The third model *introduces* a third financial market: that for non-monetary indirect assets which *are issued by* a group of non-monetary financial intermediaries that *purchase* business bonds. In a final chapter the governmental monetary system *is replaced by* a private banking system, and the quantity of money outstanding *reflects* profit considerations of the private banking system, which *is* subject to control by a central bank.

(Total talk about 1,700 words.)

4.3 A parallel-passage writing exercise based on a passage from the Introduction to *Econometric Techniques and Problems* by C. E. V. Leser (Charles Griffin & Co. Ltd.). (Total talk/text 1,200 words.)

(a) The following sentences are read and their construction is noted carefully.

There have been earlier studies which we would nowadays describe as econometric, notably the pioneer works of Moore (1914, 1917). Nevertheless it is true to say that the subject is still in its infancy, and while a substantial body of econometric research has been carried out, there is still a great deal of work to be done before many of its results can be considered as well-established.

(b) Then the sentences are re-written keeping the same construction but changing the vocabulary items indicated below (remembering to make any necessary changes in singular/plural verb agreement).

studies/research
econometric/sociological
notably/particularly
pioneer works/later writings
Moore (1914, 1917)/Weber (1916, 1918)
subject/research
infancy/early stages
substantial/considerable
body/number
econometric research/preliminary experiments
well-established/quite conclusive

Expected answer:

There has been earlier research which we would nowadays describe as sociological, particularly the later writings of Weber (1916, 1918). Nevertheless it is true to say that the research is still in its early stages, and while a considerable number of preliminary experiments *have** been carried out, there is still a great deal of work to be done before many of its results can be considered as quite conclusive.

(* *has* is also possible)

4.4 *Mathematical Expressions*

1 The expressions are listened to and attempts made to write them down.

2 The answers are compared with those on the answer sheet.

3 The expressions are verbalised by the students and the attempts either compared with model answers on tape or with written representations of the symbols.

Examples

Symbols

(1) x^2 x^3 x^4 x^6

(2) $\underline{x}'$ $\underline{x}'''$ $\underline{x}^{-1}$ $(\underline{x}'\underline{x})^{-1}$

(3) $\tilde{x}$ $\hat{x}$ χ^2 $\bar{x}$ x^* $\bar{\bar{x}}$

(4) $\sum_{t=1}^{n} y_t$ $-\infty \int^{\infty}$

(5) $(ax)^2$ $[ac-bd]/e^2$

Verbalisation

(1) x squared; x cubed; x to the fourth; x to the sixth.

(2) x dash, or x transpose, or x prime; x triple dash; x inverse; x dash x, inverse.

(3) x tilde; x hat; chi squared; x bar; x star; x double bar.

(4) sigma from t equals one up to n, yt; the integral from minus infinity to plus infinity.

(5) ax all squared; ac minus bd all over e squared.

4.5 *Caution and Approximation.* Based upon two pages in *Leading Issues in Economic Development* by G. M. Meier (OUP).

(1) The following sentences are read by the students and the fact that they are all definite statements is noted.

1 The emphasis on national independence through 'inward-looking' policies, and the advocacy of policies to avoid 'foreign domination' become part of an ideology that is called the economics of discontent.

2 'Inward-looking' policies run counter to economic development.

3 Industrialisation is viewed (by underdeveloped countries) as a superior way of life. Rich countries are rich because they are industrialised.

4 When the rural sector is prosperous the non-rural sector is large and also prosperous.

(2) The students are then instructed to read the relevant pages of

their book and note the difference in the sentences as written above and the sentences as written in their book. They are asked to copy the sentences, underlining the parts which have been added or changed. The sentences from the book are reproduced below with the verb form indicating caution in italics.

1 The emphasis on national independence through 'inward-looking' policies, and the advocacy of policies to avoid 'foreign domination' become part of an ideology that *might be* called the economics of discontent.

2 'Inward-looking' policies *are most likely to* run counter to economic development.

3 Industrialisation *tends to be* viewed (by underdeveloped countries) as a superior way of life. Rich countries are *believed to be* rich because they are industrialised.

4 When the rural sector *tends to be* prosperous the non-rural sector is large and also prosperous.

(3) A number of other sentences from the book are then selected and the students are asked to modify them in a similar way to that shown above i.e. to render them less definite.

4.6 *Style and mode.* Formal, written definitions of economic terms are taken from *The Penguin Dictionary of Economics* and are modified so that they are suitable for use in the informal, spoken mode. The students listen to this version, noting the important elements. Later they see a written representation of it and cross out the obvious colloquialisms. They then write a formal definition and later compare it to a written version. The informal and formal versions are compared and commented on. Further practice is given by taking other definitions and treating them in a similar way (e.g. macroeconomics; econometrics).

Example: What is microeconomics?

(a) spoken: informal (colloquialisms are underlined)

Yes, well, um ... microeconomics is, *I suppose*, about the study of the individual 'decision units' – *you know*, the consumer, households, and firms and so on. Also, of course, the way in which their decisions interrelate to determine relative prices of goods and factors of production, *oh yes*, and the amount of these which will be bought and sold. *As we all know*, the final aim of microeconomics is to understand the mechanism which allocates the total amount of resources which society has among all the different uses. *It goes without saying* that the most important *thing* in microeconomics is the market. *That should do: I don't think I've left anything out.*

(b) written: formal
Microeconomics is concerned with the study of the individual 'decision units' – the consumer, households, and firms, the way in which their decisions interrelate to determine relative prices of goods and factors of production, and the quantities of these which will be bought and sold. Its ultimate aim is to understand the mechanism by which the total amount of resources possessed by society is allocated among alternative uses. The central concept in microeconomics is the market.

(From: *The Penguin Dictionary of Economics*)

REFERENCES
I am grateful to Mr K. James, Department of Education, Mr P. F. Leeson and Miss Eileen McDermott, Department of Economics and Miss Jillian Taylor and Dr J. L. Bridge, Department of Economics and Social Statistics, University of Manchester for their help in the compilation of this paper.

10

Study Skills in English: Theoretical Issues and Practical Problems

C. N. CANDLIN, J. M. KIRKWOOD AND H. M. MOORE

What follows is an account of one approach to a practical problem of course design with an examination of the issues that arose in the planning and implementation of the course itself.

1 Initiatives for the Course

In 1971 we were asked to provide a three-week intensive course in English for post-graduate students coming to Britain under the aegis of the British Council to undertake post-graduate study. We discovered that the majority of the students would be in Britain for at least one and possibly two academic years. In most cases the terminal award would be a master's degree. The manpower and material resources at our disposal determined the possible scope of our activities and the British Council was informed that we could take 40 students and would run four specialist groups. The final choice of subject area was determined on the basis of data supplied by the British Council in terms of the distribution of foreign students over a range of specialisms. From this information it seemed sensible to concentrate on *Engineering*, *Economics*, *Urban Planning* and what became known as *Foreign Service*, a term for the training undertaken by overseas postgraduate students who were embarking on a career in the Foreign Service of their respective countries. Having chosen the subject areas we then requested the British Council to send us only those students who were going to study in one of those fields.

2 Course Design Problems

As with all courses, the design and implementation of *Study Skills in English* involved dealing with the following problems:

190

1 Deciding on syllabus content
2 Designing a course programme
3 Assessing students' ability
4 Working within the constraints of time and available resources

The first two of these areas at first glance might appear to relate to theoretical issues in that decisions are approached from the basis of a course designer's beliefs and theories about the nature of language. Solutions, as a result, are likely to vary widely. The other two areas, on the other hand, seem more practical and straightforward, simply inevitable factors to be considered when mounting any particular course.

Figure 1 : A model of course design

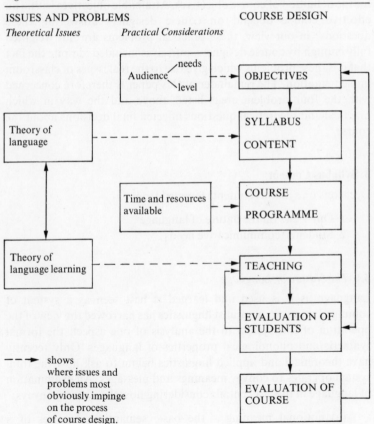

ISSUES AND PROBLEMS   COURSE DESIGN
Theoretical Issues   *Practical Considerations*

- - - ► shows where issues and problems most obviously impinge on the process of course design.

What is more important, however, to the professional curriculum planner is that these areas are not discrete areas for decision, able to be approached independently of each other. For Hooper (1971) course design is 'an interactive process where each problem is constantly being reprocessed in the light of answers to subsequent questions'. (p. 122) A model of course design needs to show that although each section has its own intrinsic issues, the outcome of the whole process (i.e. the course as actually taught) derives from a consideration of each section in relation to the others.

Evaluation of the effectiveness of a course needs to take into account the combined effect of all factors insofar as these relate to final assessment of the students. In this paper we shall be suggesting that the interrelation of the so-called practical areas of pragmatic decision with more fundamental theoretical issues raises important questions for the definition of course objectives. Attainable objectives within an effective course depend on course designers answering these questions; in our view, these practical problems are not weighted fully enough by course designers, ourselves included, despite the fact that it is these problems which give rise to the real issues of classroom implementation. The remainder of this paper is therefore concerned with the four problem areas listed above and the way in which practical and theoretical questions affected final decisions about the course.

3 Syllabus Content

Decisions on syllabus content stemmed from:

1 Our views on the nature of language
2 Students' communicative needs

3.1 *The Nature of Language*

Language as it is used and learned is best seen as a system of communication. Structuralist linguistics has narrowed the view of the operation of this system to the analysis of one aspect, the formal syntactic and phonological properties of languages. Only recently have theoretical and applied linguistics begun to ask how the total system operates to convey meanings and messages. An examination of language in this way entails considering how the system conveys:

(a) notional meaning – the basic semantic categories of a

grammar – (e.g. how notions of Time, Place and Quantity are conveyed)

(b) propositional meaning
(c) contextual meaning
(d) pragmatic meaning

As an example of how these four types or levels of meaning are conveyed, we can consider the following text:

(1) 'The end of the bipolar postwar world' has been acknowledged by the latest presidential State of the World message. Although it is elliptic in describing the new design for a lasting and stable 'structure of peace', there is little doubt that the blueprint for the future is inspired by the past. It is the model of the balance of power which moderated, if not the aspirations at least the accomplishments, of rulers in the eighteenth and nineteenth centuries. It restrained violence (without curtailing wars). It provided enough flexibility to ensure a century of global peace after the Congress of Vienna, despite drastic changes in the relative strengths and fortunes of the main actors.

from Stanley Hoffman 'Weighing the Balance of Power'
Foreign Affairs Vol. 5, July 1972, p. 618.

3.1.1 BASIC SEMANTIC CATEGORIES

Taking first a notion that is fundamental to probably all semantic systems, it can be seen that *time-related meanings* are realised in a variety of word-classes and structures:

(2) *end*; *post*war; *has been* acknowledged; *latest*.

Under the same notional heading we find a heterogeneity of form. This has implications for the way in which data such as the above are presented to the learner and organised for his learning, a point which will be taken up below (3.1.5). A notion more central to this particular passage is the *'conflict'/'peace'* dichotomy. Here again a variety of lexis and structure is used to denote these notions; further, and possibly more importantly, we find that the semantics of other lexis and structures have become related to the central 'peace'/'conflict' notion by virtue of their association together in this particular passage:

(3) *items denoting notions of 'peace' and/or 'conflict'*	(4) *items related 'by association'*
bipolar	presidential
postwar	State of the World
peace (2)	lasting
balance of power	stable
moderated	structure of [peace]
restrained	blueprint
violence	model
wars	aspirations
	accomplishments
	rulers
	curtailing
	flexibility
	drastic changes
	relative
	strengths
	fortunes
	actors

The foreign learner has to master, not only the denotative and connotative value of the items in column (3), but also he has to see how the semantics of the items in column (4) can be drawn 'into the ambit' of the 'peace'/'conflict' semantic.

In practice, this means that in order to read effectively and to write correctly and fluently, the learner has to be very much aware not simply of the relationships between meanings but, most importantly, of how words collocate:

e.g.
   (5)   the bipolar world
   (6)* the bipolar earth
   (7)   the ... design for a lasting and stable 'structure of peace'
   (8)* the ... pattern for a lasting and stable 'structure of peace'
   (9)   the model of the balance of power which moderated, if not the aspirations at least the accomplishments, of rulers ...
 (10)* ?the model of the balance of power which lessened ...

It will be noted that the collocations marked * may, in some cases, be quite acceptable in other disciplines: (6) is presumably feasible in the register of 'natural science'.

3.1.2 PROPOSITIONAL MEANING

In order to approach the meaning of, for example, the first sentence of this paragraph, the foreign learner has not only to understand the semantics of the words and phrases of which it is composed: he has also to grasp what Austin (1962) called the locutionary force of the utterance, that is, what is predicted by the utterance or what can be loosely called its information content. This requires an understanding of how a sentence is built up to express a proposition which, for the first sentence of passage (1) above, could be very informally represented as:

(11) X [the end of the bipolar postwar world] has been acknowledged by Y [the latest presidential State of the World message].

or

(12) Y [...] has acknowledged X [...].

Here, understanding the relationship between the grammatical subject and other functional elements in a sentence is crucial. In complex sentences, grasping this is very often dependent on seeing what we have termed *NP/VP unity* that is, the hierarchical syntactic relationships in a sentence.

3.1.3 CONTEXTUAL MEANING

The paragraph under discussion is the first paragraph of an article on International Relations. Introducing context entails an examination of how utterances pattern together in sequences and how any one utterance has a value in relation to what it presupposes and what it entails. In relation to this point, Widdowson (1973) makes a crucial distinction here between *text* and *discourse*.

An analysis of 'text' reveals the way in which sentences interconnect and cohere grammatically. So, for example, the reader has to be aware of the anaphoric reference of the various *its* to *the ... message* and *the model of the balance of power* (as well as the use of extraposed 'it' in line 5). Furthermore, there is a significant textual connection between the lexical items 'message' and 'blueprint for the future' which the reader has to grasp.

The 'discoursal' analysis examines how utterances realise such functional categories as, for example, hypothesis or refutation. It would appear that just as in conversation there are distinct patterns which can be isolated, for example how individuals open and close talk, how they interrupt, how they force repetitions of information and the like (Sinclair, Coulthard et al. 1973; Schegloff, 1968; Jefferson, 1972), so in written texts, including EST tests, repetitive rhetorical patterns can be observed: a proposition opens, is exemplified with evidence, the evidence estimated, a counter-proposition is forestalled, further exemplification is given, an opinion (overt or covert, tentative or direct) is delivered, and a conclusion made. It is then part of the meaning of a sentence how it relates formally and functionally to the other sentences in the text which contains it. In the example paragraph, consideration of the first sentence in its context makes clear that the information about the contents of the president's speech is offered by way of sounding the theme of the article. It is possible to isolate the focal point of the sentence as the word *bipolar*. Understanding the meaning in context enables the reader to focus on certain aspects of the literal information content of the sentence: the literal meaning has 'value' as a message from writer to reader only if its place in context is understood.

3.1.4 PRAGMATIC MEANING

Analysis of pragmatic meaning involves going beyond the context provided by the discourse itself to introduce Speakers and Hearers interacting as participants in a particular setting and possessing certain real world knowledge. The analysis asks questions about the speaker's/writer's attitude to what he is saying and to his listener/reader. In the first sentence of the example paragraph, it can be seen that the writer is not interested in U.S. foreign policy as such – the intention is not to inform, criticise, shock or amuse but rather to indicate that the president's phrasing of a statement is a significant 'straw in the wind'.

3.1.5 LANGUAGE AS SYSTEM

It has been suggested (3.1) that an analysis of language as it conveys meanings crosses the boundaries and classifications of linguistic data set up by structuralist linguistics. Further, new variables are considered relevant, namely those which relate to the context as created by the discourse, to the conventions which operate in particular types of discourse and to the real-world context in which discourse takes place. If, as we have maintained (3.1), language is fundamentally a system of communication, then the learner needs to be able to understand and use it in terms of how meanings are communicated. We would, in our situation therefore, argue against the grading and selection of learning items in a syntactically orientated progression. Rather, the implication is that the syllabus should be organised around 'items' of meaningful communication (see Pit Corder 1973, pp. 298 ff for a useful discussion of 'learning' items) and that these items should be exploited to draw out aspects of the four types of meaning discussed above. Especially in what is essentially a remedial course, we do not want to subject the learner merely to a faster run-through of grammatical structures: what he needs is to become attuned to the ways in which he can reorganise and extend what he has already learned.

3.2 *Students' Communicative Needs*

The problem of defining language content within 'English for Special Purposes' has been seen in terms of three stages: defining 'general English', defining the 'English of Science', and defining the numerous Englishes of 'specialist sciences'. Such a hierarchy poses considerable descriptive difficulty of a data-collecting and analysing kind, and we are certainly not at the point where, notwithstanding the results of the *OSTI Report* (1968) and the work of Ewer, Hughes-Davies and others in Chile (1971, 1972), course writers have such differentiated data awaiting didacticisation. Indeed, it may be that analyses such as the above, which have rested on lexical counts and surface structure listing in a classical registerial framework, have not thrown up so many differences between the three stages mentioned above as one might have expected. That is certainly the view taken by Corder (1973), which is not to say, of course, that analyses which rest on a view of register seen in terms of varied communicative function might not throw up considerable differences. Indeed, the notion of communicative *purpose* implies such differentiation and could not be accommodated under any 'general English' label. We can only pose the problem here that there may be as many 'Englishes of special purpose' as there are disciplines expressed in English; without an agreed basis for analysis and much more data no general answer is possible. In a similar way we cannot answer categorically the question of the existence of a common core of language to be mastered before specialist language courses begin. Ewer (1974) suggests such a core can be established at beginner level. It is still open whether it could be established at the more advanced level of a pre-*Study Skills in English* course. Recent work on 'threshold language within the Council of Europe (Trim et al., 1973) suggests considerable elasticity in core-size.

Our position on the language content of the *Study Skills in English* is clear; the data for learning derive, as nearly as possible, from the actual language of real settings for which our students need English. Real settings are important for students to test out their use of language; such settings imply:

1 Close approximation to the type of study setting awaiting the student.

2 A genuine communicative purpose for the student, i.e. a setting in which the participant does not feel himself merely to be playacting future roles (or worse, playacting implausible future roles) but being engaged in using language to communicate what *he* considers worthwhile messages at that particular point in time.

In order particularly to meet this second point, our course was very much activity-based. Teaching centred around preparation for a given activity or post-activity analysis using video- and audio-tape recordings, for example of tutorials led by outside tutors from the students' own fields. To meet the first point, we began our course preparation by seeking as much detail as possible on the courses offered by the institutions to which our students were going, linked to our own professional assessment of the learning settings facing graduate students from overseas.

It is in meeting these two points that course designers first meet conflict between their beliefs about the nature of language and practical realities. Clearly the use of authentic language data and settings becomes increasingly more impracticable as one's audience becomes more heterogeneous in terms of study goal. We have already indicated at the outset of this paper the four study areas within which we work (Economics, Engineering, Urban Planning and Foreign Service); despite this limitation it is clear that *Engineering* itself subsumes a possible variety of 'Englishes' – how much more difficult it is then for course designers who cannot insist on even that degree of homogeneity when attempting to provide the learner with the date of 'language in use' to meet his needs.

3.3 *Study Skills Analysis*

In our analysis of study skills and how these relate to linguistic skills we have proceeded from the reasonable assumption that any one 'study situation' requires more than one 'linguistic skill'. In other words, we maintain that the lecture, seminar or private study 'situation' will require the student to employ more than one linguistic 'skill'. Furthermore, we have attempted to analyse the four primary 'skills' of reading, writing, speaking and listening (rightly defined by Corder as 'epiphenomena' or gross labels referring to a complex of ill-understood psychomotor and psycho-linguistic processes) into lists of 'subcomponents' of skills, without claiming to have been in any sense scientifically rigorous. We established what we might' term a series of 'macro' skills which we related to study 'modes', as shown in the diagram below.

MODE:	Lecture	Seminar	Tutorial	Private Study
SKILLS	a) Listening comprehension	a) Listening comprehension	a) Listening comprehension	a) Reading comprehension
	b) Note-taking	b) Note-taking	b) Note-taking	b) Note-taking
	c) Ordering points in a hierarchy of importance	c) Oral delivery from / notes / without notes	c) Oral delivery from notes / without notes	c) Ordering of points in hierarchy of importance
				d) Formal (academic) writing, report writing

Each of these macro skills was further analysed (notionally) into micro skills which allowed us to plan the activities of our course and select appropriate linguistic data. 'Reading', for example, was differentiated in three ways: 1) *extensive* reading (reading quickly while achieving general understanding), 2) *intensive* reading (reading carefully to establish meaning in complex, usually highly technical text), 3) *skimming* (reading for the purpose of deciding whether a given article, book, etc. merits close attention). As the diagram above suggests, each study mode required the student to draw upon a subset of 'micro' skills which in turn were always drawn from more than one of the 'epiphenomena' *reading, writing, speaking, listening.*

We decided, therefore, that since our students would be engaged in activities in their postgraduate courses, and since these activities would require subsets of skills, our programme should consist of components which would help students to engage in relevant activities requiring appropriate skills. Such a decision, as we shall now see, had far-reaching implications for the structure of our course.

4 Course Programme

We can list the main components briefly. These were:

A *Specialised Topic Groups*

These corresponded to the four major fields of postgraduate study, namely Economic/Business Studies, Foreign Service/International Relations, Engineering, Planning. Specialist topic group activities took up by far the major part of the course. Each group took part in a number of different types of sessions, namely:

1 Seminar sessions: reading comprehension and associated exercises.

2 Language laboratory sessions: note-taking, close listening exercises, pair-work.

3 Televised seminar sessions: two sessions on specialised topics led by staff from the particular disciplines.

4 Project and case-study sessions: problem solving 'games'.

Details of some of these sessions are given in the Appendix to this paper.

B *Remedial Groups*

Here students were allocated to groups on the basis of types of learners' errors and not in terms of their specialist field of study.

C *Individual Tutorial Sessions*

This type of session allowed tutors to discuss the problems of individual students to hand back work and to give advice.

D *Assignments*

Students were expected to do a considerable amount of private work, much of which was essential for later class-work.

E *Orientation Sessions*

These formed a $2\frac{1}{2}$-day block at the beginning of the course and served to introduce students to the type of activities they would be engaging in during the main course.

F *General Lecture Sessions*

Our major design problem was to integrate these components into a meaningful structure best suited to realise our objectives. An example of how we attempted to solve this problem is reproduced in the following diagram. As can be seen, the diagram shows a series of interlocking events, which required the students to engage in a wide range of activities. Each activity was motivated in two ways: *firstly* by its relevance to the future needs of the student, *secondly* by the preceding activity which was the input and the next activity which

General Session   *Practice Activities*   *Simulated Situations*

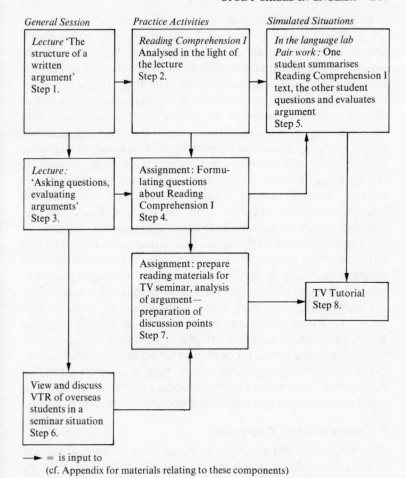

→ = is input to
(cf. Appendix for materials relating to these components)

was the output. We decided, namely, that activities on the course itself should be, as it were, interdependent, that no one activity should seem to be an end activity in itself but that each should arise out of some preceding activity and serve as an indispensible input into a future activity. Central to our thinking was the concept of cyclicity. We decided that the chief study 'modes' should rotate so that students would come back again and again to the same sort of demands made upon them by the conditions of a given 'mode' and that there should be a 'back-up' service of practical class-work and private study sessions which could serve as preparation.

In general we believe that our design is reasonably successful, although we are aware of several disadvantages. One is that such a design requires extremely careful pre-planning. We have to begin with the first session and plan each session right through to the final one, long before the course even starts. The disadvantage is that we thereby remove flexibility, the possibility of changing the structure at the last moment, or indeed of 'fine tuning' the running of the course once it has begun. A second disadvantage is that, unless the students have a very clear idea of the purpose of the design and also a proper understanding of its complexity, they rapidly become confused. If this happens, however inadvertently, the reason for the design is negated, namely that of making the students aware of the interdependence of linguistic skills on the one hand, and the interdependence of linguistic skills and study modes on the other.

To counteract this confusion we have introduced a two and a half day 'orientation session' which seeks to introduce the students to the design of the course, its purpose, and examples of the types of activity in which they will engage. This session has been largely successful.

Furthermore, as we have now run the course for three or four years, we are becoming aware of the need to slightly vary the emphases which we have hitherto placed on different study modes. We are becoming aware, for example, that we need to include a well-organised remedial component, that we need to allow more time for private study, that we may need to introduce a form of 'streaming' as a first step towards a more individual approach to student demands.

5 Constraints on the Programme

The two most important constraints are those of time on the one hand and level of proficiency on the part of the students on the other.

5.1 *The Constraints of Time*

The fundamental question which has to be answered somehow is 'how much can be achieved in three weeks?' This is perhaps an unscientific formulation, but the question is still fundamentally important. Clearly we assume that *something* can be achieved, but attempts to define 'something' either qualitatively and/or quanti-tatively raise in turn a whole series of questions to which there are no objective or valid answers.

We have come to the conclusion that what students can certainly achieve is a greatly improved insight into their own individual learning problems, sharpened by their foreknowledge of what demands will be made upon them in the future, together with a degree of confidence in their ability to handle future study situations. We regard this as a not unimportant achievement. In terms of measurable improvement in their ability to 'read' or 'handle grammatical structures' or whatever, we have simply no way of knowing whether our course is successful or not.

Certainly we feel that we have tried to include too much in the programme, in the sense that there is very little 'unprogrammed' time. We suspect that a reduction of organised group sessions in favour of more 'self-study' periods might build in a degree of flexibility which would allow students more opportunity to tackle their own specific learning problems. We also feel that we have neglected somewhat the importance of providing fast and accurate feedback to the students in relation to their efforts. A decision to remedy this in the future will of course necessitate the sacrifice or reduction of some other part of the programme.

5.2 *Establishing Proficiency Levels*

Here we continue the discussion of the issues raised in 5.1, since the question of time constraints is bound up with other constraints relating to pre- and post-testing as well as on-going monitoring.

We have, frankly, not solved the problem of predicting with much accuracy the level of proficiency which could be regarded as a 'common denominator' in relation to the total audience. Attempts to do this in the past have failed, usually for the well-known reason that valid and objective tests have not yet been devised for testing 'performance' which includes combinations of complex skills. In other words, there are no objective tests which will allow one to establish accurate notions of performance levels. A consequence of this is that we are regularly faced with the problem of accommodating students on the course whose actual performance levels fall far below those which we have taken for granted.

We have to decide then whether to advise the students not to take the course or devise some ad hoc way of constructing a programme which is more suitable for them. The former course of action is usually difficult for various diplomatic reasons, and the latter course is not very satisfactory.

Indeed we have reached the point where we are beginning to wonder whether our course does not make unrealistically high demands on our students. We are perhaps in danger of producing a course for an audience which does not exist, or if it did, for an audience who would not require this type of course.

We feel the need for three fundamental changes in the course as it is conceived at present. Firstly, we need to establish a reasonably rigorous feedback control system (e.g. we need a series of built-in tests with rapid feedback to students). Secondly, we need to incorporate a more sophisticated remedial strand which is delicate and sensitive to varied and changing student demand. Thirdly, we need time to build up a large store of varied but relevant remedial teaching materials, ideally indexed and catalogued according to type of difficulty.

These are major changes and might (probably will) radically alter the structure of the course as we have it at this time. We believe, however, that we can still teach to basically the same design, while possibly limiting the activities required of the students both in range and degree of difficulty. In other words, we would not depart from our fundamental belief that it is possible to use 'real data' and stimulate relevant opportunities for students to practise activities which will be required of them in their postgraduate work.

6 Appendix

In this section we include some sample exercise material from the main components of the course programme outlined in section 4 above.

6.1 *Specialised Topic Groups*

(a) READING COMPREHENSION EXERCISES

The students were each given copies of an article which had been set as preliminary reading for a tutorial they would later have with an outside tutor in their own specialist area. Accompanying the article was a set of comprehension questions divided into two sections, Section A which aimed to develop skimming skills, and Section B intended as a deep reading exercise (see above page 199). The students were instructed to read through the Section A questions before starting the passage and to ask for clarification if the questions were not clear to them. The questions were simple True/False questions and could be answered with a fairly superficial reading of the passage; most of them fall within the category of 'literal' questions as proposed by the Barrett taxonomy. The title of the passage was also discussed.

Pre-reading and discussion of the Section A questions and the title of the article aimed to develop in students a sense of reading for a specific purpose. They were instructed to read the passage as quickly as possible, simply looking for the answers to the questions and nothing else, i.e. their task was to find out whether the passage substantiated or denied a number of statements. This replicated as closely as possible one of the main reasons for which students might wish to use skimming techniques. It was also often necessary to give some brief instruction regarding the avoidance of vocalisation and the possibility of increasing eye span width. It must be admitted that training students in skimming techniques was very difficult, especially at our level and with the type of text difficulty they encountered: the students tended to be perfectionists and the prose was often turgid. In our experience it took a great deal of practice and a good deal of 'moralising' on the tutor's part to persuade students that it was not a crime to subject a text to one's own purposes, i.e. to read it to extract simply the information that one wanted from it.

Having completed and corrected Section A (the faster students correcting themselves by re-reading the text), the student began Section B: deep reading. The questions in this section utilised the Barrett taxonomy and ideas from Mackay and Mountford (1972) in their design.

(b) PARAPHRASE EXERCISES

The third step (usually a separate session) was what we loosely termed 'paraphrase'. This could focus on any of the areas discussed in section 3.1 above. To give an example, the following sentence might form the basis of discussion:

> Even if both dogma and growing power should push Peking toward a global role, given its internal problems the transition will be long, and China is bound to remain in the meantime a potential super-power, i.e. a major player presently limited in scope but exerting considerable power globally.
>
> (Stanley Hoffman ibid., p. 620)

Questions which relate to intra-sentential function and NP/VP unity are as follows:

1 At what point in the sentence would you divide it in two?
2 Taking part 1:
   (a) At what point would you divide it in two?
   (b) Where would you make another division?
   (c) What is the main clause?
   (d) What structures introduce the sub-clause?

    (e) Make up a sentence using the first sub-clause marker plus a main clause.

    (f) Make up a sentence using the second sub-clause plus a main clause.

    (g) Make up two sentences of the same type as (d) and (e) with different sub-clause markers.

    (h) Make up two sentences with the same meaning as (d) and (e) but with different structures.

3 From 'a major player ...' to the end:

    (a) What points in the sentence can be expanded using *which*?

    (b) What other words have to be added if *which* is used?

A syntactic/semantic paraphrase question:

4 Re-express the following phrases keeping the meaning the same but changing the structure if necessary:

push Peking toward a global role

the transition will be long

in the meantime

is bound to remain

presently limited in scope

exerting considerable attraction

These questions can hardly claim to be revolutionary: their main claim is that they relate to structural and semantic problems that the student is going to have to face in this and similar texts. They are aimed to present the student with a strategy for dealing with complex syntax as well as to bring to light the particular problems posed by this specific sentence. Presented as they are above, they appear rather bald. In fact, they represented a strategy for class discussion rather than a set exercise which the student had to work through on his own. Question 2 (f) for example, gave rise to considerable discussion and experimentation towards the precise structural and semantic function of *given* as a subordinator: what was its logico-semantic function? – could it be replaced by other subordinators syntactically/semantically? Similarly, Question 4 raised problems of audience, role and channel for discussion.

(c) VOCABULARY EXTENSION

An exercise which largely concentrated on the issues raised in 3.1.1 is as follows:

(the first paragraph of the text to which these questions relate is given in 3.1)

1 (a) What nouns in this passage are related in meaning to the noun *model* as it is used here?
       (Expected answers:
       design, blueprint, system, policy, structure)

   (b) What verbs are used with these nouns? e.g. 'the model *moderated* ... the accomplishments of rulers.'
       Give other examples in this way.
       (probable answers:
          the blueprint is inspired ... the past.
          the model restrained violence.
          the model provided flexibility.
          „   „   is in favour.
          „   „   is tempting.
          the system is coming to an end.
                        ... etc.)

   (c) Use the word *model* in sentence of your own on this topic.

2 (a) Pick out all the words and phrases in paragraph 3 that are to do with *types of relationships between states*.
       (probable answers:
          balance-of-power
          a contest of actors
          ambitions ... have to be contained
          by the power of other states' equilibrium
          fixed blocs
                        ... etc.)

   (b) Use one of these words/phrases in a sentence of your own on the same topic.

The main problem with these types of questions was that they did not provide the student with enough opportunity for practising the structures and lexis discussed. This problem could be complicated by differing ability levels within a class. In this case we were confronted with the problem of reacting sufficiently quickly and effectively to learning difficulties. This could be solved by building up a bank of supplementary exercises, but as yet time and manpower have precluded this.

A further difficulty is also evident: it was easy for the student to do well in a class run on the above lines and yet retain very little at the end. So far, we have given insufficient attention to follow-up from one lesson to the next. This problem could be fairly easily overcome by giving short and frequent tests.

(d) DISCOURSAL EXERCISES

It will be noted that *Reading Comprehension I* is preceded by a lecture on '*The structure of written argument*', (p. 201). A handout (see p. 210) exemplifying and expanding the points made regarding discoursal meaning accompanied the lecture and was applied to the reading text (see Step 2 of diagram p. 201). Exercises which concentrated on discoursal meaning were of the following general type:

   I   Students label sentences or parts of sentences according to headings such as *hypothesis, qualification, exemplification* etc.

  II Students provide explicit linguistic markers for the rhetorical patterns to be found in a text.

III Students underline topic sentences.

IV Students sum up each paragraph of a passage in a sentence or phrase, and then rewrite their summary in a connected paragraph.

(e) QUESTIONING STRATEGIES

Reading Comprehension 1 was followed by a lecture '*On Asking Questions and Evaluating Arguments*'. (See handout p. 210.) The points covered in this lecture were applied in a later class (see step 4 of diagram p. 201) and again as part of the preparation for a language laboratory session. The following *Assignment Exercise* based on *Reading Comprehension I* is set as preparation for the language laboratory, and also indirectly for the T.V. tutorial:

1 Imagine that, after reading this article, you were to have a seminar with the writer:

   (a) Make up one question for paragraphs 2–8 that you would like to ask him.

   (b) After you have made up these questions, refer to the handout 'On Asking Questions in Seminars'. What is the function of each of the questions you have made up?

   (c) Use the examples given in the handout to make up one question for paragraphs 9–17.

   (d) Use the examples in the handout to make up one more question for paragraphs 2–8. The function can be the same as your original question but the way you express it must be different.

2 Tomorrow, in the language laboratory you will have an opportunity to discuss this article with a colleague:

   (a) List five topics you think might be discussed with your colleague.

(b) Formulate a question to put to your colleague about each of these topics.

(c) What is the function of the questions you have formulated?

(d) Make up two more questions with a function different from those you have already formulated.

This exercise was designed not only to sharpen the students critical abilities but also to highlight the way in which role relationships can effect both the function and formulation of questions. The exercise moves from a fairly straight-forward imaginary situation where the student probes the writer about what he has written (here one expects the student to be largely concentrating on making his doubts and criticisms of the article explicit) to a more complex activity: the student probes a fellow-student about his reactions to what they have both read. In shifting from the first situation to the second (and one supposes that the student would initially regard this as a relatively trivial change), the student should become aware of a shift in style and function, that is, of how doubts and criticisms can be formulated differently.

(f) PAIRWORK EXERCISES (LANGUAGE LABORATORY) (see Step 5 of diagram p. 201)

It might be of interest to give a few details regarding the language laboratory activity to which the above exercise (together with a summary exercise) acted as input. In the language laboratory the student tape recorders were adapted to allow two students to record onto one tape deck. (Many modern laboratories have this facility; failing this, junction boxes can be made up fairly easily.) The students' brief was a suitably elaborated version of that given on page 201 (Step 5). They discussed for five minutes or longer, wound back and monitored what they had done, making a critical appraisal of their discussion and questioning techniques together with the tutor. This kind of work has proved to be an extremely valuable follow-up to reading and written work in that it provided students with a context in which they had to draw extensively on material (and therefore lexis and probably structures and rhetorical techniques) that they had met in their reading. As a language laboratory exercise, pair work has the advantage of involving all students simultaneously in discussion – no one can opt out as is possible in class discussion. This type of exercise requires skilful, efficient and intensive monitoring by the tutor and some experience in phasing each pair's rewind and monitor steps; also students need to be encouraged to be critical of themselves and each other (e.g. the tutor monitors something that fairly obviously requires comment; the students pass it by; the tutor stops the tape elicits rather than directly makes the comment, and then says something to the effect of 'Well, why didn't you stop the tape and discuss this yourselves?'; he then lies in wait for the students to pass something else by, and repeats the same performance. In other words, the tutor's technique is to make it obvious to the students that part of the activity is self-monitoring). A further advantage of this type of activity, in terms of the course structure, is that all students had a chance to discuss the topic before the T.V. tutorial class and should therefore have felt reasonably familiar with the topic and how it might be discussed.

6.2 *General Lecture Sessions*

The following are two sample handouts from these lecture sessions; the first with *patterns of argument in written texts*, the second deals with the language of *asking questions in seminars*. Students are expected to use these handouts as cues to their own oral and written performance, and they are also intended to indicate to the student useful ways of organising language data for communicative learning.

EXAMPLE 1: PATTERNS OF ARGUMENT IN WRITTEN TEXTS (see Step 1 of diagram p. 201)

Section One: Framework: *The structure of a written argument*
PATTERNS OF ARGUMENT IN ENGLISH
Written arguments in specialised English frequently take one of the following two forms:
A: 1 Evidence cited
2 Evidence estimated
3 Opinion given (Agreement or Disagreement) $\pm$ Tentative/ $\pm$ Overt
(Opinion may be challenged: *actually* in Spoken Argument, often *anticipated* in written argument)
4 Opinion upheld or modified (i.e. Challenge answered)
Here is an example of the above type A:
As a starting point A assumed B
He further hypothesised C
To test his ideas he did D and E
Despite his second step he did ...
A principal achievement of A's study was ...
In my judgement the weakest link in A's study was K

Of course this is the result of H

But nevertheless A failed to do L

B: *An alternative pattern of argument takes this form:*
1. Opinion given: ±Overt/±Tentative (Possibly Agree/Disagree with what has preceded)
2. Evidence cited
3. Evidence estimated
4. (Opinion may be challenged: see above)
5. Opinion upheld (restated) or modified (i.e. challenge answered)

Frequently spoken argument takes the second form B, in that one's personal point of view may take first place, and challenges can be expected at any point during the presentation. Written formal arguments of particular cases or hypotheses frequently take form A, and here challenges, or what the writer regards as possible challenges (counter-arguments, alternative views etc.) are presumed in order to forestall critics.

The major difficulty is that each of the stages in argument suggested above can be realised by a large number of phrases and formulae in English. There are many ways of stating evidence, for example, and one can present opinions more or less overtly, more or less tentatively. One can agree or disagree more or less directly, one can assert more or less forcefully.

SUGGESTED PHRASES/FORMULAE FOR THE ABOVE STAGES OF ARGUMENT

1 CITING AND ESTIMATING EVIDENCE

We have already stated there is disagreement concerning X

There are sharp contradictions between ...

X states the view that ...

The point made by X is that ...

X's writing would lead us to think that ...

In putting forward X's points we should not forget that ...

The earliest view on A is X's that ...

Similar views have been held by C, D, D ...

No definite conclusions can be drawn from ...

The theories of X seemed to be confirmed by ...

X assumed that ...

X's ideas were accepted and developed by ...

X is the basis for Y's contention that ...

X became widely accepted at the time of B ...

Before we do X we must do Y ...
X is generally accepted. This implies that ...
On present evidence (see X, Y, Z) it must be argued that A is B
NOTE ALSO THAT DIRECT QUOTATIONS MAY BE MADE
FROM SUPPORTING EVIDENCE

NOTICE HERE THE CONNECTION TO THE LANGUAGE OF
LOGICO-GRAMMATICAL CATEGORIES – ESPECIALLY
THE LANGUAGE OF HYPOTHESIS AND CAUSE/RESULT

2 *GIVING PERSONAL OPINION*

In order to avoid continuing repetition of personal involvement in
particular opinions (that is to avoid stating: I think this, I hold this
view, In my opinion this should be done, etc., etc.) writers frequently
use phrases which are intended to appear to be reflecting the opinions
of a group of which the actual author is a part, but which may in fact
be only the opinions of the author in question. We can call these
COVERT EXPRESSION OF PERSONAL OPINION.

This last suggestion may be readily accepted
This surely is understandable
One would also find it difficult to see ...
One gets the impression ...
This certainly is novel
While this is true ...
It would surely be going too far if one say ...
It has surely gone beyond ...
One may well wonder
You are not logically compelled to do X and Y
One's verdict would depend on one's attitude of mind
It is widely felt
... will receive general approval
One may underline the connection
One may perhaps take it that
This certainly is a move in the right direction
This must, however, be read with caution
One should have expected X to mention Y
It is not uncommon
It is often sensible
It should be reiterated
It is assumed that
It is apparent that
It has been shown that

It might be thought that
It is to be supposed that
It is considered that
It is proposed that

VERY FREQUENTLY THIS COVERT EXPRESSION OF
PERSONAL OPINION TAKES THE FORM OF A PHRASE
BEGINNING: IT IS ... YOU SHOULD REMEMBER THAT
OFTEN THESE 'IT' PHRASES CAN BE REPLACED BY A
SIMPLER FORM, WHILE STILL STAYING COVERT.
It is clear that ... clearly
It was noted that if ... if
It was obvious that ... obviously
It was observed that molecules which ... molecules which
It has a tendency to ... it tends to
Take into consideration ... consider

ANOTHER METHOD OF STATING PERSONAL OPINION
COVERTLY, ESPECIALLY IN WRITTEN ARGUMENT, IS TO
USE PHRASES LIKE:
In the opinion of the writer/author: the author holds the view that ...
We feel that etc., etc.

SECTION TWO: Personal Intentions and Views.
e.g. *Agreement and Disagreement*
As with all expression of personal intention and views, there are often
strong differences between the *language of oral expression* and the
language of writing. Furthermore, expressions can lie along lines of
formality/informality and *certainty/tentativeness*.

Agreement/Disagreement may be more or less qualified, more or
less tentative
(A) *AGREEMENT*
   I am in total agreement with X when ...
   I agree totally/completely with X ...
      absolutely/entirely
   I believe implicitly that what Y states ...
   There can be no objections to Y's ...
   Undoubtedly Y ...
   Y definitely makes the correct point when ...
   There seems little doubt that/It seems wholly possible that
   More QUALIFIED Agreement
   If we agree X then Y must follow

X is true but Y doesn't follow

X is true but there is no evidence for Y

X is true but we must also consider Y – therefore Z is doubtful

Although I agree with X, I wonder if Y

Although X is generally true there are exceptions like Y

This seems very acceptable but we must take Y into account

I absolutely agree with X but I am worried above Z

(B) *DISAGREEMENT*

I cannot agree with X when ...

I am in disagreement with X when ...

I could not possibly hold the views of X

It is not possible to maintain X's view that ...

X must be wrong when ...

There is no doubt/undoubtedly X is incorrect when ...

I find it difficult to agree with X when ...

I am particularly worried about X's view that ...

I cannot see how one can go along with X when ...

More QUALIFIED Disagreement

X says Z, but I say ...

You say X but I ask ...

They say X but/evidence says ...

          I say ...

                 I wonder if I could say/it could be said ...

I think X is assuming Y but I say this is doubtful

I understand X but I cannot agree/hold that view/maintain that position etc.

EXAMPLE 2: ASKING QUESTIONS IN SEMINARS
(see Step 3 of diagram, p. 201)

1 *Basic question types:*

		Example
(a)	YES/NO interrogatives:	Can you begin to see ...
		Excuse me, may I return to ...
		Have you seen that sentence before?
		Has this just been discovered?
		Do you really think ...
(b)	WH-interrogatives:	What is your opinion on ...
		What is your view concerning ...
		How do you compare ...
		How would you show that ...
		Which would be the given information ...

(c) disjunctive interrogatives: Would one use this proof or is there another method?

Does this always happen or are there exceptions?

When would we apply this formula, or is it not used any more?

Can one say that or does it not depend on the circumstances at the time?

How would we demonstrate that, or is that not important?

(d) tag questions: You don't do it like that, do you?

We can't use this method, can we?

Network analysis isn't the same as PERT, is it?

Sewerage and sewage disposal are the same things, aren't they?

It doesn't follow from that that X = Y, does it?

(e) echo questions: What did you say this theory proved?

What did you say Chomsky's definition is?

Chomsky says what?

(f) 'hidden' questions: I don't suppose one could say that.
(= Could one say that?)

I understand A, but I don't see how B fits in.
(= How does B fit in?)

Perhaps we might go over that again sometime.
(= Can we go over that again sometime?)

I was very interested in what you said about X, although I didn't understand Y.
(= What about Y?)

2 *Basic functions of questions*
  (a) to obtain confirmation/refutation (YES/NO)
  (b) to elicit explanation/clarification

    (c) to elicit new information
    (d) to elicit corroboration
    (e) to elicit repetition
    (f) to imply agreement/disagreement
    (g) to challenge implicitly/explicitly
    (h) to refute implicitly/explicitly

3 *Possible modes of expression:* questions phrased
    (a) politely
    (b) impolitely
    (c) formally
    (d) informally
    (e) tentatively
    (f) directly
    (g) persuasively
    (h) etc.

4 *Example: Asking for repetition*

INTERRUPTOR		REQUEST
NON-VERBAL	VERBAL	
+	Excuse me,	I seem to have missed the point, mind going over A again?
+	I'm sorry,	
+	Sorry,	I'm not clear about A. Would you mind explaining it again?
+	—	
—	Excuse me,	Would you mind repeating that, please?
—	I'm sorry,	Could you please repeat that?
—	Sorry,	Would you please run through that point again?
—	—	What did you say Chomsky's definition is?
—	Eh!	Why do you think Fillmore is wrong?
		What did you say about focus?
		What did you say?
		Chomsky says what?
		Suppose what? etc. . . .

(The left margin is labelled vertically TENTATIVE ↓ DIRECT; the right margin is labelled vertically TENTATIVE ↓ DIRECT.)

5 *Example: Asking Academic Questions*

Question: $\square + \triangle - \diagup\!\!\square = \bigcirc$?

    (a) Is that formula true in all cases? (1a, 2a, 3a, c, f)
    (b) I may be dense, but I don't see that, I'm afraid. (1f, 2b, 3a, d, e)

(c) That can't be true in every case, can it? (1d, 2d, 3a, d, e)
(d) You're not asking us to believe that this formula actually works, are you? (1a, 2c, 3a, c, f)
(e) Could you explain, please, what the applications of this formula are? (1a, 2c, 3a, c, f)
(f) I'm sorry if I appear confused, but does this formula have practical applications, or is it merely of theoretical interest?
(g) This formula is applicable to what? (1e, 2e, 3b, d, f)
(h) What would be the result of applying this formula to Z situation? (ab, 2c, 3a, c, f)
(i) I find this formula fascinating from a theoretical point of view but don't see any obvious applications of it. (1f, 2c, 3a, c, e)
(j) If this is true we make the following conclusion? (1a, 2d, 3a, c, f)

6 *Problems*
  (a) overlapping categories of function/mode of expression
  (b) lack of clear criteria for describing each category
  (c) need for accurate analysis of stress and intonation (both in relation to function of question, and also in relation to mode of expression)
  (d) need for analysis of context – what are the relevant facts?

6.3 *Remedial Groups*

The following is a sample of remedial reading comprehension material designed to improve students' ability to grasp the conceptual and rhetorical structure of a written text. It was developed for the *Study Skills in English* programme by Jonathan Leather, one of the tutors on the 1974 course. (Cf. also Leather, 1974.)

The student first read the text below. He was then asked to draw lines (to show connections) and arrows (to show specifically causal relations) between the boxes. Thus, lines should link the three physical phenomena of 'sun', 'water' and 'wind' to the conceptual heading, 'weathering and erosion'. An arrow from, say, 'sun' to 'expansion' shows the causal connection stated in the text. The text is as follows:

Weathering and erosion include all the processes by which rock is worn away and its debris removed to be deposited elsewhere. The bizarre shapes of desert pinnacles, sea-shore cliffs and glacial valleys bear witness to the effects of sunlight, wind and water. Often it is not so much the water itself (its volume and force) which sculpts these effects, but the particles and chemicals that it carries along. Water-borne acids eat the rock away. The sun heats up certain grains in the rock faster than others, and the different expansion rates result in crumbling stresses. Strong winds carry particles over the landscape, dumping them in water and abrading all in their path. A flake of mica, a quartz sand-grain scours even a rocky river bank a million times as it swirls downstream. Tiny deposits of water in a crack or crevice freeze, expand 10 per cent, and crow-bar the fissure wider.

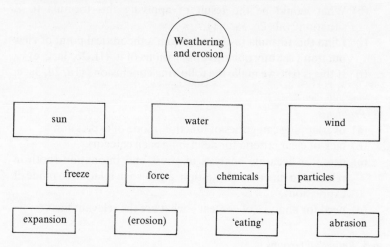

REFERENCES

Austin, J. L., *How to Do Things with Words*, Oxford University Press, 1955.

Barrett, Thomas C., 'Taxonomy of the Cognitive and Affective Dimensions of Reading Comprehension', unpublished paper; see Clymer, T. 'What is reading?: some current concepts.' In Melnik, A. and Merritt, J. *Reading: Today and Tomorrow*, University of London Press Ltd., in association with the Open University Press, 1972, pp. 48–66.

Corder, S. P., *Introducing Applied Linguistics*, Penguin, 1973.

Ewer, J., 'Integrated Programming for STTE,' mimeo Department of English, University of Chile, Santiago, 1974.

Ewer, J. R. and Hughes-Davies, G., 'Further notes on developing an English Programme for Students of Science and Technology', *English Language Teaching*, Vol. 26, No. 1, 1971 (65–70) and Vol. 26, No. 3, 1972 (269–273).

Hoffman, Stanley, 'Weighing the Balance of Power', *Foreign Affairs*, July, 1972, pp. 618–643.

Hooper, R. (ed.), *The Curriculum: Context, Design and Development*, Oliver and Boyd (Edinburgh) with the Open University Press, 1971.

Huddleston, R. D., Hudson, R. A., Winter, E. O. and Henrici, A., *The*

Linguistic Properties of Scientific English, London: Communication Research Centre, Department of General Linguistics, University College, London, 1968 (The OSTI Report).

Jefferson, G., 'Side Sequences' in Sudnow, D. (ed.). *Studies in Social Interaction*, New York Free Press, 1972.

Leather, J., 'Theme Schemes', M.A. Project, University of Lancaster, Department of Linguistics and Modern English Language, 1974 (mimeo).

Mackay, R. and Mountford, A., 'A Programme in English for Postgraduate Students in the Faculties of Sciences, Applied Sciences and Agriculture at the University of Newcastle on Tyne', *ASLA/AIMAV*, Conference Stockholm, 1972 (mimeo).

Schegloff, E. A., 'Sequencing in Conversational openings', *American Anthropologist*, 70, 6, 1968.

Sinclair, J. and Coulthard, M., *Towards an Analysis of Discourse*, Oxford University Press, 1975.

Widdowson, H. G., 'Directions in the Teaching of Discourse', in Corder, S. P. and Roulet, E. (eds.). *Theoretical Linguistic Models in Applied Linguistics*, Brussels, AIMAV and Paris, Didier, 1973.

Proper Name Index

Index